Few leaders have the conviction a[n]
compelling book like this. Rhys Ste[nner] ...uc.s anu aiso exudes compassionate leadership with pastoral care in helping others wrestle through the toughest questions in life. Get this book. Share it with others. Let this thinker stimulate your mind, will, and emotion to live your life with living faith.

Dr. Ronnie Floyd, President, Southern Baptist Convention,
Senior Pastor, Cross Church, Springdale, AR

This challenging new book, *If in Doubt*, makes it possible for us to navigate the turbulent seas of scholarship and science as well as the storms of skepticism and searching. This book is well written, with real-world illustrations, hard-hitting facts, and interactive questions throughout. Rhys Stenner will help all who read it to discover the wonder of the Creator, the grand narrative of history, and personally experience the peace of being fully convinced in their own minds. I have spent my life trying to prepare students for those moments where everything they believe and have been taught is under attack. This book allows all who read it to find safety in the harbor and to put down an anchor that will hold.

Dr. Jay Strack, Founder and President,
Student Leadership University

The application of biblical truth has been "field tested" in the marketplace by our family business Chick-fil-A for over seventy years. My dear friend Rhys Stenner in his book *If in Doubt* summarizes the fundamental truths that will light the path for those of us willing to embark on a spiritual journey determined to find answers to the questions we secretly ask along the way. Resolving these questions brings joy, peace, and freedom to perform at our highest potential!

Dan T. Cathy, Chairman and CEO, Chick-fil-A

Having doubt is normal. Staying in doubt is not. Rhys Stenner's book will help you move from the desert of doubt to the fields of faith from the world's beginning to your ending. Enjoy the journey!

James Merritt, Lead Pastor, Cross Pointe Church,
author of *52 Weeks with Jesus*

I am so glad that my friend Rhys Stenner has given to us the gift of *If In Doubt*! You will find this to be a practical, treasured resource for all of us who are either searching for answers or ministering to those who are. Thank you, Rhys, for giving us straight, clear, and biblical answers to some common as well as tough questions.

Dr. Crawford W. Loritts Jr., Author, Speaker, Radio Host
Sr. Pastor, Fellowship Bible Church, Roswell, GA

My friend Rhys Stenner has written a powerful resource for all Christians on dealing with doubts that show up during their faith walk. There is no question that, at times, we all struggle with biblical truths, and it is imperative to understand God's Word and God's heart in the midst of those struggles. This book, *If In Doubt*, gives us all hope as it reveals God's desire and plan to answer not only some, but all, of our doubts.

Jonathan Falwell, Senior Pastor,
Thomas Road Baptist Church, Lynchburg, VA

My friend Rhys Stenner has written an excellent book to help anyone facing doubt. For seasoned believers who are helping others process their questions, this is an incredibly helpful resource. Or for seekers and new believers trying to find answers to some of the most common questions about faith, Rhys's insights are simple and straightforward. This book will help to break down barriers and open avenues of communication for gospel conversations. A wonderful resource full of biblical truth!

Michael Catt, Senior Pastor,
Sherwood Church, Albany, GA

All of us at times have had spiritual doubts. Someone has said that if we feed our faith, our doubts will starve. Rhys Stenner has given us a menu of faith that helps us turn doubt into dependence. This book presents biblical answers to skeptical doubt. Dinner is now being served. Come hungry!

Ken Whitten, Senior Pastor,
Idlewild Baptist Church, Lutz, FL

Rhys expounds on some of the most basic tenets of our faith . . . and he knows how to tackle the hard stuff! *If in Doubt* is for those strong in the faith or questioning their faith. It is chock-full of answers to questions you may have been afraid to tackle yourself or talk to others about. This book is a breath of fresh air to the dry and weary land of doubt.

Dave Stone, Pastor,
Southeast Christian Church, Louisville, KY

Rhys addresses the doubts many Christians struggle with at one time or another. By masterfully weaving Scripture with personal accounts, he identifies and answers the tough questions for you. *If in Doubt* is a useful disciple-making tool for new believers and growing disciples alike. Read this book. You'll be glad you did.

Robby Gallaty, Ph.D., Senior Pastor,
Long Hollow Baptist Church, Hendersonville, TN

If we are honest we've all had some honest doubts on our journey of faith! That's why I am so excited about my friend, Rhys Stenner's encouraging book, *If in Doubt*. Stenner tackles the difficult questions that believers and nonbelievers encounter when facing the claims of Christianity, and he provides answers to help all who are on an intelligent faith quest. A life-changing book for all who search for eternal answers!

Dr. Dwight "Ike" Reighard, President/CEO, MUST Ministries,
Senior Pastor, Piedmont Church, Marietta, GA

If in Doubt gives simple yet profound answers to what seems to be the most asked questions about God and the Bible. Place this book in the hands of a new believer and arm him in biblical defense, or place with the unbeliever and answer his skepticism.

Johnny Hunt, Pastor,
First Baptist Church, Woodstock, GA

Everyone struggles with doubts about God from time to time. Yet, thankfully, when we learn to doubt our doubts and talk with God about our struggles, He strengthens our faith. Rhys offers concrete insight that helps us all in dealing with our doubts. This is a book you don't want to miss—not only for yourself but also for friends who are struggling with doubts.

Bryant Wright, Senior Pastor,
Johnson Ferry Baptist Church, Marietta, GA

Pastor Rhys Stenner shares the gospel message in a way that is simple and life changing. As you read this book, you will experience the keys of the kingdom of God open before your eyes. All you have to do is listen with your heart!

Lee Haney, eight-time Mr. Olympia
Past Chairman to the President's Council on Fitness
Founder of The International Association of Fitness Science

In a world influenced and motivated by an ever-changing worldview, *If in Doubt* provides a clear, accessible, and practical response based on the foundational truths of Christianity. This excellent and transformative book is useful for anyone exploring core ideas for a Christian worldview. Pastors, teachers, and small group leaders will find this book helpful for individual and group study.

Tim Woodruff, EdD, Associate Pastor, Discipleship,
New Hope Baptist Church, Fayetteville, GA

IF

IN DOUBT

RHYS STENNER

IF

IN DOUBT

ANSWERING THE SEVEN
GREAT QUESTIONS ABOUT FAITH

WORTHY®
PUBLISHING

Published by Worthy Books, an imprint of Worthy Publishing Group, a division of Worthy Media, Inc., One Franklin Park, 6100 Tower Circle, Suite 210, Franklin, TN 37067.

WORTHY is a registered trademark of Worthy Media, Inc.

HELPING PEOPLE EXPERIENCE THE HEART OF GOD

eBook available wherever digital books are sold.

_____

Library of Congress Cataloging-in-Publication Data

Names: Stenner, Rhys, author.
Title: If in doubt... : answering the seven great questions about faith / by
    Rhys Stenner.
Description: Franklin, TN : Worthy Publishing, 2016. | Includes
    bibliographical references.
Identifiers: LCCN 2016004859 | ISBN 9781617957567 (tradepaper)
Subjects: LCSH: Christianity--Essence, genius, nature--Miscellanea.
Classification: LCC BT60 .S74 2016 | DDC 239--dc23
LC record available at http://lccn.loc.gov/2016004859

_____

Unless otherwise marked, Scripture quotations are taken from THE HOLY BIBLE, NEW INTERNATIONAL VERSION®, NIV® Copyright © 1973, 1978, 1984, 2011 by Biblica, Inc.® Used by permission. All rights reserved worldwide.

Scripture quotations marked ESV are taken from the ESV® Bible (The Holy Bible, English Standard Version®) copyright © 2001 by Crossway, a publishing ministry of Good News Publishers. ESV® Text Edition: 2011.

For foreign and subsidiary rights, contact rights@worthypublishing.com

Published in association with Ted Squires Agency, Nashville, TN.

ISBN: 978-1-61795-756-7

Cover design: Faceout Studio, Derek Thornton
Interior Design and Typesetting: Bart Dawson

Printed in the United States of America
16 17 18 19 20 21 VPI 8 7 6 5 4 3 2 1

To LOUISE, MY WIFE. This book has taken thirty years to write, and you have walked with me in ministry the whole time. Thank you for your love, prayers, and sacrifice. You are a fine thinker and teacher, and a wonderful wife and mother. Thank you also for not claiming the credit for the best ideas in the book, which we all know are yours! I love you!

To OUR CHILDREN—Megan, her husband Alex, and baby Brynlee; Eleanor; and Sarah. You have been the biggest encouragers for this book. You believe in the truths represented here, and each of your specific insights has fired me up again and again.

To ALL OUR FAMILY for moving to the United States, never complaining, adding two more to our family so far, and cheering for the same team. You bring me so much joy.

To OUR CHURCH FAMILY at New Hope for receiving us and treating us like your own. Thank you for being good listeners and doers of the Word, for caring for each generation, and for supporting this book with gusto. We love you. This book was originally inspired by New Hope's incredible students.

CONTENTS

FOREWORD

BY DR. JACK GRAHAM

Even if you truly believe in Jesus Christ, you may have many questions about life, death, faith, the Bible, and the future. Doubt is a problem for many Christians.

Yet doubt is a necessary element of faith. Let me explain. Faith does not mean that you have all the answers to every question but that you believe in the God who does have all the answers. Faith is trusting God even when you have questions you can't answer—and even when there are things you don't understand.

Faith, at its core, is believing what you cannot see. Jesus said to the apostle Thomas after the resurrection, "Have you believed because you have seen me? Blessed are those who have not seen and yet have believed" (John 20:29 ESV).

My good friend Rhys Stenner faces these doubts head-on. In the pages of this book, he addresses the most important doubts and fears that Christians often have. *If in Doubt* will help you believe your beliefs and doubt your doubts and discover a living faith that will not only give reliable answers to many of your questions but also provide a strong foundation for your faith.

Both seekers and skeptics will appreciate Rhys's honest, thoughtful, and transparent approach to doubt. In a word, as the British say, it's brilliant! *If in Doubt* is brilliant because your ifs can be turned to answers and your sincere doubt into an honest faith. You will discover truth, which is life changing.

This book is also a practical resource to help you answer questions from people who don't know God and are looking for meaning and purpose in life. Since we should always be "prepared to make a defense to anyone who asks you for a reason for the hope that is in you" (1 Peter 3:15 ESV), this book will give you solid, sincere, and scriptural support as you share the gospel.

Read this book, and you will walk away with a faith that is knowing and growing in the Word of God and the testimony of Jesus.

INTRODUCTION

A CLEAR VIEW OF TRUTH

I grew up by the sea. My dad was an officer in the Royal Navy, and my brother has worked on boats all his life. So I have a soft spot for old wooden ships, especially the ones with huge masts, sails, rigging, and cannons.

Whenever I imagine myself on one of those wooden ships, I always picture myself holding a sailor's telescope—what some call a spyglass. These old-fashioned handheld telescopes could be pulled out in sections beginning with a wider view and then revealing a more powerful focus. Perhaps you have seen a telescope like this or maybe you noticed one as you watched the Pirates of the Caribbean movies!

I want you to imagine the most powerful extending telescope that sailors could use in an old ship. It had not just three sections but seven. This book is divided into seven chapters, like a seven-section telescope. It begins with a wide perspective and then adds lenses that zoom in on the most important questions about faith. Each section is vital. Like an extending telescope these questions are linked together, so as each section is added, we can see more clearly what matters most.

FOR THOSE STRUGGLING WITH DOUBT

The popular voices in our Western culture encourage spiritual doubt and discourage Christian faith. It is trendy today to make fun of Christians and to mock the biblical worldview as old-fashioned or unintelligent. We are told that science has disproven the Bible and that mankind has advanced beyond the need for religion. We hear things like:

"How can you possibly believe that today?"
"Haven't modern discoveries disproven the Bible?"
"How can you be a Christian and still have a brain?"

This book helps answer the questions of faith, and it challenges the doubts that can be answered.

Perhaps you are struggling with doubt. You may have grown up around a committed faith, but you want to believe because you are truly persuaded, not merely because it is your background. These are the doubts of faith—that is, valid questions that can be answered to strengthen faith. Maybe you are a stranger to the seven great questions, but through this book you will become acquainted not merely with the ideas but hopefully with the One behind all of them.

In the following chapters we will push beyond what we know, pulling out section by section of our extending telescope to focus on the sharpest reality that will take us to home to the shore.

JESUS LOVES THOSE IN DOUBT

Recently I had the privilege of going to India, a nation that is home to over a billion people. Though India is full of many religions and some say over one hundred million gods, the nation also has a vibrant Christian church presence. One missionary I know has over seventeen hundred house churches under his pastoral care.

Indian believers appreciate the apostle Thomas, who is credited with founding the church in India. Thomas was a man of great courage—he was willing to travel to challenging places and to die for Jesus. But he also carries the unfortunate name "Doubting Thomas." The apostle Thomas went through a painful week of doubt after Jesus's death and resurrection. Thomas had seen much, but he had not been with his fellow disciples when the risen Christ appeared to them. So he doubted.

However, Jesus did not give up on Thomas. He loved Thomas and addressed all of his questions when He appeared in the Upper Room. Jesus showed the disciples His hands and His sides—the scars from His brutal death. The crucified one was alive, and everything changed! Doubt and misery became faith and joy. When Thomas saw Jesus clearly, he exclaimed, "My Lord and my God!" (John 20:28).

If we are in doubt, the answers may be much nearer than

we realize. But when we receive the answers, we must also be willing, like Thomas, to say that Jesus is our Lord and our God.

I, too, was caught by surprise by Jesus. As a fourteen-year-old, I thought I was a Christian because I was British. I had read the Bible and even believed it to be true, despite a growing cynicism in my nation. But I listened to the secular voices around me and began to doubt if Christianity was really true. Then I met Jesus. A punk rocker friend told me one day, out of the blue, that I was a sinner and needed a Savior. He told me why Jesus died for me. I believed and stopped doubting. My faith was set on fire.

Perhaps, like I was in my early years, you have been influenced by secular voices and doubt whether Christianity is true—or whether God even exists. After all, we hear over and over that the Bible is full of contradictions and fairy tales, right? Or maybe you are a Christian who has a loved one or friend who struggles with doubt, and you aren't sure how to respond to their questions. No matter where you are in your faith, this book is for you.

Sometimes doubt is lack of assurance in an uncertain outcome (such as whether our favorite sports team will win). Doubt can also be the result of lazy thinking or a stubborn refusal to face the facts. But doubt can also be a very good thing. Doubt can spark valid questions and cause you to investigate issues in order to uncover the truth. So if you are in doubt when it comes to the Christian faith, don't use that as an excuse not to pursue the answers you are looking for. Instead, let your doubt spur on your thinking as we explore these seven great truths.

ANSWERING THE GREAT QUESTIONS

In these chapters, we will focus on seven truths that build a solid foundation for our faith. "Faith," says Hebrews 11:1, "is confidence in what we hope for and assurance about what we do not see." When our foundation is right, we can build our faith and our lives on these solid and secure truths.

We miss the point if we think that genuine, biblical faith is about just the unknown or the unseen—in other words, a blind faith. True faith is putting our trust in what is sure and certain. No matter what, even when we have a bad day or face skeptics and critics, if we have searched out the answers to these seven great questions, then we can have a clear perspective.

I hope that all generations will use this book as a fact and faith builder. May these truths encourage us to have a full confidence and assurance in Scripture. As we pull out the sections of the telescope with each of the following chapters, my prayer is that the truths explained in this book will answer the seven great questions that are essential for a lifetime of faith.

DID GOD MAKE THE WORLD?

I was pastor of a church in Brighton, England, when I began preaching a series of messages on the book of Romans. If you are not familiar with this book in the Bible, Romans is one of the most comprehensive, theological letters in the New Testament. Many scholars say that one should not rush through preaching such a great epistle—for example, the late pastor Dr. Martyn Lloyd-Jones preached on this one letter for an incredible fourteen years! I scheduled the series for a mere twenty-six weeks.

I planned to preach through the book of Romans a few verses at time, but as I prepared my message for chapter 1, I was drawn to verse 20. I paused and read the verse again and again. I could go no further.

For since the creation of the world . . .

I was struck by this simple statement. My nation of Britain no longer embraced this truth. There was a time when the majority of British people had a strong view of God's creation. Then Charles Darwin proposed his theory of evolution. A century came and went, and attitudes about mankind's origin gradually shifted. Schools began teaching evolution as fact, and in time, almost everyone began referring to what humans used to be like when we were in more primitive form. God became less relevant to our education and our everyday lives as our nation became more heavily influenced by the theory of evolution.

Throughout the Western world, including the great thinkers and philosophers of Britain, the question of mankind's origin—creation versus evolution—was once considered a valid discussion and a fair debate. But as the years went by, the naturalist view (the belief that nature is all there is and no more) became more dominant—not because of overwhelming proof but because the majority of people began to scoff and say, in essence, "Only fools doubt evolution."

Despite the disproof of many of the so-called evolution evidences that my generation had been fed in high school, the "fact" of evolution was widely assumed and accepted in Britain. In our society, people were shamed for holding a belief that went against the majority. Those who questioned or debated the theory of evolution were treated as mentally weak. Evolution was assumed to be fact—and not allowed to be reexamined. But the evidence supporting evolution was not so forthcoming. It was like the preacher who once put in his notes, "Argument weak here; shout louder!"

Britain's educators were encouraged to teach revisionist history—a new and different interpretation of previously
assumed history. But while most of history was fair game for
revision, neither teachers nor their students were given the
intellectual freedom to reexamine the assumptions that led
to the development of the theory of evolution in the nine-
teenth century. So, for example, reexamining the history
of warfare was acceptable, but reexamining the history of
evolution in the century when Darwin developed his theory
was not acceptable.

Our culture was not looking up or to the distant land.
The telescopic sights were seen as old and redundant. The
foundation of our culture was beginning to shake.

So I preached through Romans 1, focusing on these
most vital words:

> For since the creation of the world God's invisible
> qualities—his eternal power and divine nature—
> have been clearly seen, being understood from what
> has been made, so that people are without excuse.
>
> For although they knew God, they neither glori-
> fied him as God nor gave thanks to him, but their
> thinking became futile and their foolish hearts were
> darkened. . . .
>
> They exchanged the truth about God for a lie,
> and worshiped and served created things rather than
> the Creator—who is forever praised. Amen. (vv.
> 20–21, 25)

Like those to whom Paul was writing, the people of

Britain saw God as no longer relevant to ordinary life. Most still believed in God and thought He was nice to have around, but He had nothing to do with where we came from or where we were going. In other words, the prevailing view was, "God is okay—as long as you don't let Him have His say in biology, sociology, psychology, history, or ethics, for that matter."

We were reduced to relying on basic instinct rather than reaching for the higher plane of knowing God. Like the Romans, we exchanged the truth for a lie. The result of this was materialism, the belief that we must follow our physical urges and satisfy them with material things. With this view, any restraint or self-denial suppresses our freedom to enjoy whatever we want whenever we want, and therefore it must be rejected. This materialistic mind-set was not good for our nation—and it was definitely not working.

WHY CREATION MATTERS

Some Christians in Britain preferred to ignore the problem of this widespread loss of belief in biblical creation, saying instead, "Let's just tell people about Jesus." But if there is no Creator, then there is no God, no judgment, and no need for salvation in Jesus. The question "Did God create the world?" is ultimately founded on the most basic question of all: "Is there a God?" If this foundation is lost, then we lose everything.

I was stunned throughout the 1990s as legislation changed rapidly in Britain in a way that made biblical values irrelevant, even illegal. The Judeo-Christian worldview was eroded in schools, despite most of the nation still claiming to be Christian.

While working as a pastor in Brighton, I also volunteered as a school governor. Some governors were very kind, but at times I was made to feel like a cultural outsider for believing the Bible. I tried, unsuccessfully, to suggest that everyone on the governing board had a belief in something. I am not sure, however, that such a thought could even be heard. People often claim that they do not have a religious view and are therefore objective. I have found this rarely to be the case.

Laws that had once protected children and the elderly because of our belief in a Creator God were replaced by what I call "opinion-poll ethics," subject to the ebb and flow of the latest fads and often driven by aggressive activists. Standards of taste and decency plummeted. The great Christian heritage that had helped create freedom in the West was replaced by the spirit of the age, which was governed by the one who shouted loudest. This standard brought neither freedom nor tolerance.

In our schools, educators who taught revisionist history began to say that missionaries who traveled to faraway lands to take the gospel, and along with them brought Western culture and conveniences, were bad. These revisionists also taught that Christian beliefs were dangerous and must be removed. The loudest voices in our culture began to reason that we no longer needed to listen to the law of God, since He didn't make us in the first place. After all, if everything on earth is the result of natural processes, then we don't need God. Instead, we can make our own way and define our own rules.

Some Christians responded to this cultural shift toward evolution by trying to make God's truth more appealing to the naturalists by combining the biblical truth of creation with the theory of evolution—creating a theory of theistic evolution. But this blending of ideas watered down one in favor of the other and failed to supply the rigorous philosophical challenge that the theory of evolution needed. If natural process was the only agent involved in the creation of the world and everything in it, then to try to add the Bible to this process, or to say that the teachings of the Bible somehow agreed with Darwin's theory, was to relegate the Bible to superstition.

The loss of our belief in the Creator meant:

- No God
- No standard of right and wrong
- No biblical values or commandments
- No need for a Savior
- No belief in the resurrection
- No life after death
- No hope for the future

If everything in this complex and magnificent universe came from nothing by way of natural processes, then why should our school textbooks continue to teach the view of creation? On the other hand, had evolution definitely been proven true and worthy of being the only view of our origin presented to students? I continued to study the question.

THE NATURALIST VIEW

Since many people in England doubted biblical creation, I knew I needed to address this issue with my congregation in my message on Romans 1. Without an accurate understanding of the foundational truth of creation, we would likely not believe the rest of the Grand Story. When we lose the biblical view of our origin, we begin to adopt a naturalistic view of the world in every academic discipline.

For several weeks I researched and preached that God did make the world according to His Word and that we are answerable to Him. We need this foundation. I kept studying and writing and reading all I could. As I did, I noticed acutely how many things in our culture are related to our foundational presumption of evolution or creation.

Interestingly, most people in modern culture tend to respond with skepticism or even disdain when Christians claim that something has been predetermined by God. But how freely these same people accept the idea of predetermination when it comes to addictions, gluttony, and lust— they quickly blame these behaviors on their genetics! In the popular view, our genes absolve us of responsibility for our choices because they are the result of our predetermined nature. Naturalism says we are merely creatures of instinct, helpless to control our actions. The naturalist claims that the malfunctions of the body are not due to sin or the Fall but to an evolutionary hangover. But is this idea of predetermined instinct over responsible choice true?

The more I studied, the more I was encouraged by the Word of God. I began to realize that I had accepted too much of the prevailing dogma. The reality was, the arguments for evolution and its surrounding tenets were based not on science but on philosophy. The faith that each view requires—either faith in a Creator God or faith in the lack of one—informs the conclusions we make about the evidence we see.

THE BEAUTY OF DESIGN

In my study I came across a key word: *design*. Things do work remarkably well in nature. To the committed biblicist (believer in the Bible), this complexity and beauty is due to God's intelligent design. What an incredible world we live in! What amazing creatures surround us! Look how the eagle soars, the heron dives, the whale splashes, and the dolphin cruises.

The theory of evolution claims that there is no guiding force at work in the world, directing changes in the species. All is random. Only the fittest survive. To the evolutionist, everything in this universe is a result of natural selection without a selection committee. But how could blind chance turn a single-celled amoeba into something as complex as a bat flying at thirty miles per hour, eating a thousand mosquitos an hour, while guided by a kind of sonar from its own emitted sounds?

A naturalist philosopher, who presumes that no Creator or Designer exists, has to say that our entire universe somehow evolved through random, unintelligent mutation. To the proponent of evolution, everything in this world—including the complexity of the eye, the intricate music of a bird's song, and the speed of a cheetah—evolved by chance. Add a few million years, the evolutionist says, and anything can happen.

Anything?

As I continued to study this issue, I became reacquainted with the difference between macroevolution and microevolution. All creationists and scientists accept that small changes occur within species. That is microevolution. We have evidence of minor changes in today's observable species. For example, humanity has gotten larger as our diet has changed. Cats and dogs have developed considerable variants among breeds, though they are still cats and dogs. We can manipulate microevolution within a species.

In contrast, macroevolution is species-to-species change. It is the development of one species into another despite the nonfunctional nature of irreducible complexities. It takes a huge leap of faith to believe that one species evolved into another species, because scientists have never observed this happening. Not now. Not in the fossil records. Not ever.

IRREDUCIBLE COMPLEXITY

The human body is an incredibly complex system. Have you noticed that if part of the knee is damaged, such as a torn ACL, the whole thing fails? Each person's physical body is a complex system composed of multiple complex systems. For example, your digestive system is incredibly complex. Yet here is something to consider: the individual parts that make up your digestive system have neither purpose nor function without the entire system being in place.

Chemist Michael Behe wrote about this "irreducible complexity" in his book *Darwin's Black Box*. He explained, "By irreducibly complex I mean a single system composed of several well-matched, interacting parts that contribute to the basic function, wherein the removal of any one of the parts causes the system to effectively cease functioning."[1]

If a biological system or organism cannot function without each of its parts exactly designed and placed as they are, then how could this system have evolved gradually, in fits and starts, one piece at a time over millions of years? Based on the evolutionist's principle of the survival of the fittest, any component that evolved by itself would not be sustainable and so would not survive. Complex systems would never have an opportunity to develop.

Behe explained this principle using the example of a spring mousetrap. All of the components—base, hammer, spring, catch, and holding bar—must be present together in order for the mousetrap to accomplish its function. If a mousetrap only had a hammer, for example, and not the rest of the parts, it would serve no function and thus be eliminated by the evolutionary process of survival of the fittest.

Herein is the brilliance of complexity that is irreducible: a complex system demands an architect. The creationist looks at the world and sees such an architect in Creator God. The evolutionist sees only natural selection and chance.

In *Darwin's Black Box*, Behe explained how the reality of irreducible complexity reveals a flaw in evolutionary philosophy:

An irreducibly complex system cannot be produced directly . . . by slight, successive modifications of a system, because any precursor to an irreducibly complex system that is missing a part is by definition nonfunctional. An irreducibly complex biological system, if there is such a thing, would be a powerful challenge to Darwinian evolution.[2]

One example of an irreducibly complex biological system is the human eye. Recently a friend of mine, Jake Dailey, received a concussion as a result of hitting the back of his head. For three or four days he could barely see. One aspect of his sight, the transference from the eye to the brain, was affected by swelling, and the damage to this complex machinery rendered him partially blind. How could all the intricate aspects that have to work together to create vision occur gradually by random chance? All the many parts of the human eye have to be working correctly in order to see! This is irreducible complexity. Thankfully for Jake, the swelling reduced and he regained his vision.

Is this complexity of the animal and human kingdoms a result of design, or is it the remnant of some distant celestial disaster? How can complex forms evolve successfully if every part of the new form has to fully exist before the organism gains any working advantage from it? Why would a genetic anomaly that creates a nonfunctioning portion of an eye lead to the genetic development of a creature with a fully functioning eye? The idea of natural selection falls apart when one considers irreducible complexity. Surely the concept of design rather than evolution makes more sense.

Years ago I heard someone say that it takes more faith to believe that everything came from an amoeba than from

God. Yes, indeed. Science should observe what we can see rather than speculate on that for which there is no tangible evidence. Unintelligent, blind chance cannot design complex things, not even if we waited for billions of years.

PROPAGANDA AND THE PERSISTENCE OF CREATION

By the end of my eight-week sermon series on creation, much of our congregation believed in biblical creation. Many people were converted and baptized, even though we were in England's most secular city, in the country that buried Charles Darwin among kings and queens at Westminster Abbey. I believe this sermon series prepared our church in Brighton for the era that was to come. If we can trust the book of Genesis, then we can believe all of Scripture. The truths we confirmed during this series also helped my wife, Louise, and me stand firm and raise our children according to God's Word in an increasingly secular culture.

Britain is more steeped in the theory of evolution than the United States. But naturalist pundits also dominate the debate in America—or, to be more precise, they have tried to end the debate about creation versus evolution by proposing that our schools teach evolution only. Yet despite holding intellectual and social power, naturalists in the United States have failed to convince a huge proportion of the general public. Despite all the evolutionist propaganda, many Americans persist in their strong belief in creation.

Why do people hold so strongly to the biblical view of creation? Is there a common-sense factor that many scientists are missing about where everything in our world, including us, came from?

The alternative to evolution is that God said, "Let there be light" (Genesis 1:3). When we look at a sunset and sense the presence of something greater, this is not primitive paganism. We are simply recognizing the Designer behind the design.

Evolution says there is nothing special about humans; we are just another animal species that evolved though the natural process. In contrast, the Bible says that God created one man and one woman, and all of us are descendants from the uniquely designed First Couple. In the biblical view, men and women are the pinnacle of creation. We are to care for nature and the animal kingdom, of course. The Bible calls us to care for all of creation (Genesis 1:28). But taking care of nature is not the entire reason we live, because nature is not all there is.

That God exists and that He made us are the most basic truths of life. We can choose either to lift up our eyes to God and recognize Him as our Maker, or we can look merely at what is materially in front of us and attribute it all to random chance. Our choice will determine our destiny. If you have been experiencing doubt about whether God is your Maker, I encourage you to be your own observer and inquirer of the origins of this world. Ask the tough questions. Do what I did and spend time studying this subject. But as you do, be willing to accept where the facts will lead you . . . to the answer that there is indeed a Designer and Creator of everything in this world—including you and me.

A PERSONAL EXPERIENCE WITH
THE WONDER OF CREATION

Louise and I visited the Grand Canyon in 2011. I had wanted to go there for as long as I can remember. An invitation to Phoenix, Arizona, put us within three hours of this amazing site.

The drive to Phoenix with our friends Joe and Tammy was barren much of the way—just the odd cactus dotting the roadside. I'd never seen a cactus in the wild before. Finally we were there. I don't have the words to fully describe the Grand Canyon, because you simply have to see it. We marveled at the vastness of God's creation as we looked at the mile-deep canyon leading down to the Colorado River. The human eye is unable to comprehend the scale of what we were seeing. Parts of the river are almost a quarter of a mile across; but from the top, it looked only a few yards wide.

One moment we were gazing at a vast expanse. The next minute we were acutely aware of our smallness.

Along the rail that surrounded our lookout spot, we found a small, framed plaque of various scriptures proclaiming the wonder of God's creation. The evidence of creation surrounded us as far as we could see. But before we could even finish saying, "Wow," a park ranger approached us and began passionately speaking about the millions of years it took to create the canyon. He sang the praises of nature.

I noted that an expanse as vast and beautiful as the Grand Canyon should cause us to reflect, to worship something. The natural response to such grandeur is praise. We can choose to praise nature, as this park ranger did, or we can choose to praise the Maker. We can either worship the Creator God or worship the created.

Paganism worships the natural and believes this world is all there is. Geologists used to teach that the Colorado River carved out the Grand Canyon over millions of years. But recent scientific evidence makes that theory problematic. Now, as the park ranger declared to us, scientists think some of the canyon walls were formed by being "raised up." Raised up by what? The park ranger had no answer to that question. He admitted that to date, no scientist, using only known scientific principles and data, can fully explain how the Grand Canyon came to exist. This conversation was a stark reminder to me that the opinions of man don't last long, but "the word of our God endures forever" (Isaiah 40:8).

THE WONDER OF THE WORLD'S DESIGN

To understand how the world was designed, it is helpful to understand what is called the "anthropic principle." The evolutionist Alfred Russel Wallace anticipated the anthropic principle as long ago as 1904, writing,

> Such a vast and complex universe as that which we know exists around us, may have been absolutely required . . . in order to produce a world that should be precisely adapted in every detail for the orderly development of life culminating in man.[3]

In other words, the conditions had to be just right in the

heavens and the earth or humanity could never exist. Today we hear the opposite from evolutionists—they say the universe is so big and involves so many components that life had to happen eventually.

I am no astronomer, but no one disputes that the way Earth relates to the solar system is essential for human life. Meeting the narrow parameters that support life would be like hitting a pin-dot target in the middle of our galaxy. We couldn't merely hit a glancing blow or the edge of the target. The many and diverse conditions necessary to sustain the variety of life we find on planet Earth requires a bull's-eye. Let's consider a few of the many bull's-eyes that blind chance would have had to hit precisely in order to support the existence of life on Earth.[4]

The Size and Proximity of the Sun

Most of us learned in school that life on Earth has to have certain conditions for anything to live. The entire animal kingdom can exist only in a relatively narrow temperature range. The right temperature is essential to sustaining life. So the Earth must be situated in exactly the right proximity to exactly the right size of sun in order to create a temperature range that sustains life, instead of freezing or scorching it.

In addition to a suitable temperature, most animals and plants—and all humans—need water. If the distance to the sun were farther, then the temperature of the planet would be too cool to support a stable water cycle; if the distance were shorter, then the temperature of the planet would be too warm. The other planets of our solar system could only, at best, support a narrow sample of life found on Earth.

So if the sun were either greater or smaller, or if the sun were closer or farther away, humanity wouldn't survive on Earth. Maybe there could have been a less perfect planet populated only by cockroaches and spiders, but who would want that? That humanity can coexist with whales, willow trees, wombats, polar bears, and volcanoes is beyond amazing.

Earth's Axis

Another positive factor for the existence of life as we know it on our planet is the tilt of Earth's axis. If Earth's axial tilt were even slightly larger or smaller, then the surface temperature differences would be too extreme to sustain life. As we have seen, surface temperature differences affect, among other chemical processes, the presence of water. We do not have enough space in this book to marvel enough at the amazing composition of water, but its careful design makes it one of the most unique, life-supporting substances ever conceived!

Earth's Rotation

If the rotation period of Earth relative to the sun were longer than twenty-four hours, then temperature differences between night and day would be too great to support life. If the rotation period were shorter, then the resulting atmospheric winds would be too destructive for any life to survive. The existence of life on Earth depends on the

twenty-four-hour day that results from Earth's exact rotation relative to the sun.

The Moon

What if our planet did not have the moon? Scientists have
learned that we need the moon in order for human life to
exist. If Earth had no moon, then the ocean tides would be
much smaller and affected by the sun. Without the moon,
it would be much darker at night and days would be much
shorter. Years could last as long as one thousand days. The
moon is essential to sustaining life on Earth.

Thickness of the Planetary Crust

If the planetary crust of Earth were thicker, too much oxygen would transfer from the atmosphere to the crust, leaving
insufficient oxygen in our own atmosphere to support life.
However, if the planetary crust were thinner, then the resulting increase in volcanic and tectonic activity would prevent life as we know it. I liken this to pizza: neither deep pan
nor thin, but somewhere in between.

Earth's Bodyguard

Scientists have also discovered that the planet Jupiter is
necessary for life on Earth. Meteorites would have long ago
wiped out all living things in our galaxy but for one fact:
Jupiter. Planet Earth needed another planet in our solar
system large enough and with a powerful enough gravita-
tional pull to take the hit from meteorites on our behalf.
Like a kind big brother fending off the bad guys, Jupiter
protects Earth from meteors.

THE TWO OPTIONS

We can see for ourselves that Earth, and the entire universe, had to be at just the right conditions for life to occur. So now we have two options to explain how the universe got the way it is—either everything in the universe accidentally evolved through chance, or it was purposefully designed by a Creator.

Option #1: Evolution

Here is a summary of the first choice we have: evolution.

- Once there was nothing.
- From nothing came something.
- There was a destructive explosion.
- Conditions were perfectly set for life to occur on earth.
- Life occurred.
- Life grew and adapted into the millions of species we have today by random mutation.

Considering the precise conditions required for life to occur, does that summary sound reasonable or even plausible? Evolutionists assume that the universe was big enough that the perfect conditions were bound to happen eventually. *Boom!* Like an explosion in a brick factory, a destructive calamity created the universe as we know it, sending out the planets so that they just so happened to settle exactly as they are now. It was all random blind chance. Planet Earth hit the lucky bull's-eye!

According to this option, nothing intelligent—only a destructive force—made the sun exactly the right size and set it precisely the necessary distance from Earth, which created the exact right temperature for a planet that just so happened to have a 365-day cycle around the sun in conjunction with a 24-hour-per-day spin cycle.

If the sun were smaller than it is now, it would have burned out already. If it were bigger, we would have burned up. The air on Earth has the perfect amount of oxygen for us to breathe and for plants to grow and thrive. But in the evolutionist's scenario, there was as yet no life as a result of the so-called Big Bang—just empty, dead planets for millions of years that resulted from this random explosion.

Suppose we suspend judgment for now regarding this thinking of how the perfect conditions came to be in our universe and, in particular, in our own solar system. Now the question we must ask ourselves and answer is this: Where did life come from?

Assuming that this perfect environment for all current life forms all happened by random chance, where then did life originally come from? The evolutionist has no clear answer to this question. In fact, a recent trend in modern thought is to say that since we have no explanation of how life emerged on its own in our galaxy, then the original life form must have come from outer space. Is the naturalist's theory so farfetched and impossible that he has to go to such an extreme to find a beginning for life? Creation is starting to look far more sane.

The evolutionist who claims that life originated in outer space supposes that since life couldn't have happened here, then it must have happened somewhere else and flew here! We don't know from where, of course. So the evolutionists are left with meteorites being the answer. This suggestion seems to be the current favorite among today's naturalists. But take a moment and think rationally about that option. Have you ever seen a meteorite cavity in a picture or in person? Do you have a mental image of what that crater looks like? Now imagine that a life form somehow hitched a ride on a meteor and entered our atmosphere. Do you think that life form would actually survive? No, of course not. It would burn up while entering Earth's atmosphere.

If life couldn't start on its own here on Earth, where conditions are absolutely ideal, then how and why would life come from somewhere we have never even seen? These leaps in the dark are based on the evolutionist's blind faith that life somehow sprang up by itself . . . somewhere.

Can I suggest a better way forward? Ask direct questions about the idea of naturalism. Here are some:

- Was there an explosion that set our solar system perfectly for life? Or did God say, "Let there be light" (Genesis 1:3)?
- Are the sun, planets, and moons in our solar system arranged by disaster or design?
- Did life come through space travel or creation?
- Did humans become as we are by evolution from a basic form of life?
- Did nature create nature?

Option #2: Intelligent Design
Thankfully, as we are studying the issue of the origin of the universe, we do have another choice—intelligent design.

When Alfred Russel Wallace anticipated the anthropic principle—that the world had to exist within its exact, current conditions in order for life to occur and to survive—he still held to the philosophy of evolution. As scientists have learned more and more about the remarkable alignment of so many factors that make life on Earth sustainable, so the study of "intelligent design" has also taken off.

Again this is where the debate comes down to philosophy or common sense. The evidence is exactly the same: the universe we live in provides all the exact requirements necessary to sustain life. So the question is this: Was our world designed that way, or did destructive, random, and blind forces deposit us here by chance?

The anthropic principle points to intelligent design. The world and universe are perfect for life to exist. How did that happen? The Word says, "In the beginning, God . . ." (Genesis 1:1). The Bible tells us that "every living thing" was made "according to their kinds" (Genesis 1:21). In other words, there is a specific design to the created order.

The perfect conditions for life were either an incredible accident caused by chance or designed by God.

We can see many more ways in which God's creative design is on display in our world. Thank God for the ozone level, the oxygen in the atmosphere, and the molecular structure of water and carbon. The atom is almost a world within itself. That humans can breathe is a marvel. That gravity does not squash us or that we don't float away is one of many miracles of intelligent design. We can see Jupiter with the naked eye. God made it big enough to preserve life on our planet!

All of these factors speak to creation and not random chance. There are plenty more of these principles for sustainable life that we know of so far. There are probably even more that we don't know.

Intelligent design lines up with what we observe in the world. And the Bible gives the best explanation for that design. The Bible declares from its very outset, "In the beginning God created the heavens and the earth" (Genesis 1:1).

OUR GREAT FOUNDING FATHER

In addition to the book of Genesis, let's look at two verses from the middle of Scripture regarding the subject of our origin. The book of Jeremiah encourages a foundational view of creation:

> This is what the LORD says, he who made the earth, the LORD who formed it and established it—the LORD is his name: "Call to me and I will answer you and tell you great and unsearchable things you do not know." (33:2–3)

From this passage we learn that the Lord made the earth (v. 2). It was neither blind chance nor an accident but made deliberately by a designer. The Lord God is the person behind the Grand Story of our existence. He not only wrote us into the Grand Story, but He also supplies the power to sustain us. Colossians 1:17 tells us that "in him all things hold together." He cares for us.

We also see in Jeremiah 33 that the Lord "formed" the earth (v. 2). A few chapters earlier, in Jeremiah 18–19, God described Himself as a potter, forming clay in His hands according to His will. The Lord Jesus during His time on earth was also a craftsman, working as a carpenter alongside Joseph. So the Godhead—Father, Son, and Spirit—skillfully crafted creation. God formed the world as a potter forms a clay jar.

Next, we observe that the Lord "established" the earth (Jeremiah 33:2). Like a founding father, God instituted the earth's beginning. He is the Founding Father of the earth.

What does it mean to institute a beginning? It's like establishing a new nation. Years ago Louise and I had the privilege, along with several fellow pastors, to tour the Capitol building in Washington, D.C. We were led throughout the chambers by a tour guide and saw the chapel where two thousand statesmen and citizens used to attend worship services each week. (Belief in God was undoubtedly a part of the establishment of this nation.)

During the tour, we learned about how the United States of America came to be. Of course, my fellow pastors teased me for being British. We heard stories of all the bad things the Brits did, for which I am truly sorry! I did have some fun with the team, though, when I saw the statue of Winston Churchill, who was half American and a great British prime minister. I suggested everybody salute.

The point is that the nation of America was founded. It did not spring up of its own accord, nor did the Constitution write itself. Men planned and designed and created a new nation with a new form of government. The United States exists as it does now because designers planned and formed and, through sacrifice, established it.

Ultimately, God is the founder of nations because He is the founder of everything (Romans 13:1). He is the Founding Father of all nations. He established the world. He created the principles and laws of the universe and the hopes of man. It was not a disaster or an accident. Our universe, and everything in it, was gloriously planned and established by our Creator. God has especially shown interest in the earth and in people, sending His Son to this tiny, insignificant planet. Jesus came to this little spot, to us.

In Jeremiah 33, we learn the name of this designer: "The LORD is his name" (v. 2). We were not created by nature but by God, the Lord. The earth makes no sense without Him. Jeremiah also tells us that the mystery of the earth is known in God (v. 3). God is the key. Deny God and we lose perspective. Being without God is a dangerous place to live.

WHY DID GOD CREATE US?

The Bible never clearly says exactly why God created the earth—just that He did. There are certainly scriptures from which we can deduce that the purpose of creation was for His glory:

> The heavens declare the glory of God;
> the skies proclaim the work of his hands.
> Day after day they pour forth speech;
> night after night they reveal knowledge.
> (Psalm 19:1–2)

> For from him and through him and for him are all things.
> To him be the glory forever! Amen. (Romans 11:36)

Creation declares the glory of God, and humanity is the pinnacle of creation. This is an accepted interpretation of Scripture throughout most of church history. So it follows that God must have some purpose in creating us. The Bible story emphasizes the salvation of the human race as God's primary concern. So we need to know Him and be right with Him. Jesus came ultimately to die and rise again for us who live in this little place.

So let His Word speak and settle this question in your mind. Let there no longer be any doubt: God made the world, and He made you to seek Him. Believe the beginning of the Grand Story. Believe the evidence, and believe His Word.

> In the beginning God created the heavens and the earth. . . . And God said, "Let there be light," and there was light. (Genesis 1:1, 3)

> Then the LORD God formed a man from the dust of the ground and breathed into his nostrils the breath of life, and the man became a living being. (Genesis 2:7)

> The Son is the image of the invisible God, the first-born over all creation. For in him all things were created: things in heaven and on earth, visible and invisible, whether thrones or powers or rulers or authorities; all things have been created through him and for him. He is before all things, and in him all things hold together. (Colossians 1:15–17)

By faith we understand that the universe was formed at God's command, so that what is seen was not made out of what was visible. (Hebrews 11:3)

You are worthy, our Lord and God,
    to receive glory and honor and power,
for you created all things,
    and by your will they were created
    and have their being. (Revelation 4:11)

We have pulled out the first section of our extending telescope. God exists, and He created the world. Now we have a new question to answer: Should God's creation of the world affect how we live? Get ready to see a little farther.

IS THERE A RIGHT AND WRONG?

I love a new gadget—any new gadget. Louise has kindly given me fun Christmas presents over the years such as a battery-powered mini helicopter, toy racecars, and even a spy car guided by my iPhone!

But I rarely do well with these gadgets. I am not sure I have had a watch for more than a few years. I confess that I am poor at working a new contraption. I tend to try making it work without consulting the instructions. Honestly, it does not go well, especially if I miss the bits that say, "You will destroy the whole thing if you touch button C." Frankly, most directions are in minuscule print and are not written for someone as technologically challenged as me. So it feels easier to start without them.

Yet in many walks of life, it is wise to listen and learn and consult the instructions first. It saves time! If our beginning is sound and we have the correct view of creation—that God made the world—then the logical conclusion is that our

Maker also has a good plan for His creation. That good plan includes all of us. The God who made us is also the God who directs and empowers us.

The second section of our extending telescope, then, is that God has revealed His will—His instructions—to us. And since He has revealed His will, we can know that there is a right and wrong. God speaks. He is holy. We were made to know Him. If we can follow His lead, then it will go well for us ultimately. It all comes down to knowing Him and obeying Him.

WHO DECIDES RIGHT FROM WRONG?

Let's assume for a moment that there is no Creator. If there is no Creator, then there is no Maker, no revealed will, and most importantly, no authority for deciding what is right and wrong.

Those who reject the Bible are often very dogmatic about their presumption that there is no such thing as definitive right or wrong. This is nothing new. By the third chapter of the Bible, people were already choosing to ignore and defy what God said (Genesis 3:6). As a result of Adam and Eve's sin in the garden of Eden, the world changed.

Christians believe that right and wrong are revealed to us in the Word of God. Our Designer kindly gives us instructions—much better and more encouraging ones than the baffling instructions that come with my gadgets!

How can someone who rejects the Bible be sure of what is right and wrong? Who decides what is right? Do we rely on our own opinions or on the latest ideas or on what is currently acceptable in our culture?

If we follow the logical conclusion of those who reject the Bible and believe instead that everything exists as a result of random chance, then we should say to all parents: "You cannot possibly believe in the existence of right and wrong. All your efforts to challenge or train or discipline your children are oppression. You are like a dictator harming your children with an arbitrary set of traditional rules that only make them miserable. You must end the oppression now. Lower your standards. Let the kids figure it out."

In one sense, that is the message the secularists must adhere to if they are going to be consistent in their beliefs. Without a standard to guide them, there is no right and wrong. But surely loving parents don't want their children endangering themselves or growing up to be selfish or destructive. Love and discipline do not have to be mutually exclusive, do they?

My friend Dr. Joshua Straub talks about the tension that parents have as they parent toddlers. On one hand, they need to allow healthy exploration, but on the other hand they also need to intervene with loving parental protection.[1] It is a tension that parents know all too well.

God is the same. He gives us great freedom. But He also has revealed boundaries that are for our protection. Sadly, greater griefs follow when we ignore God. The key is to stay in what I call God's "circle of protection."

Let me propose the second focus for seeing life through a healthy lens. There is such a thing as right and wrong— because there is a God who reveals Himself and His ways.

In the early years of World War II, a little-known Oxford University professor named C. S. Lewis was asked to do a series of broadcasts on BBC radio. Here is how he began his first live radio show in 1942:

> Every one has heard people quarreling. . . . "That's my seat, I was there first." – "Leave him alone, he isn't doing you any harm." – "Give me a bit of your orange, I gave you a bit of mine" – "How'd you like it if anyone did the same to you?" – "Come on, you promised."[2]

Justin Phillips, in his book *C. S. Lewis at the BBC*, added,

> The point Lewis makes is that each of us appeals to or falls back upon a standard of behaviour to which we hold others to account. We may call it decency or fair-play or morality. The point of a quarrel is to prove someone else is wrong and you are right. This makes no sense unless both sides have some agreement of what is right and what is wrong, just as a foul in football, for instance, means nothing unless both sides are playing to the same rules.[3]

There is a right and wrong, just as sure as we have a left and right hand.

In this chapter, we are going to see that this sense of right and wrong ultimately comes from on high. We can know right and wrong by revelation, not by random chance or the quirks of history. If creation changes everything, if the Bible is right about our origin, then we had better quickly get back to the instructions we have received from our Maker.

PLURALISM

While I was growing up in the UK, we had one TV and three channels. Today we have many devices with scores of options and channels. We live in a world of choices. That is often our challenge. In today's culture we also have multiple options for morality, and the loudest national opinion seems to prevail. But are opinion polls the best way to determine right from wrong?

Jesus asked this question too:

When Jesus came to the region of Caesarea Philippi, he asked his disciples, "Who do people say the Son of Man is?"

They replied, "Some say John the Baptist; others say Elijah; and still others, Jeremiah or one of the prophets."

"But what about you?" he asked. "Who do you say I am?"

Simon Peter answered, "You are the Messiah, the Son of the living God."

Jesus replied, "Blessed are you, Simon son of Jonah, for this was not revealed to you by flesh and blood, but by my Father in heaven." (Matthew 16:13–17)

In this passage we see that we must make a decision about which authority to trust. All around us there are many opinions, often conflicting, about which authority we should follow. This was true in Jesus's time as well. But the apostle Peter put his trust in the revelation from heaven revealed in Jesus Christ. He trusted the supreme surety over the shifting sands of culture and time. Peter built his life on the foundation of Jesus.

When Peter first met Jesus, he responded by falling at Jesus's knees and said, "Go away from me, Lord; I am a sinful man!" (Luke 5:8). He understood that God had set a standard of right and wrong—and he knew that he fell far short of God's divine standard. Similarly, our feelings or popular opinion do not give us an excuse to reject God's standard. Right is right and wrong is wrong, as sure as your right and left hand do not change positions.

OPINION DOES NOT CHANGE THE TRUTH

You may have heard people say, "Perception is reality." Yes, what we perceive certainly seems powerfully real to us. But truth is true, regardless of what we say or feel. For example, my favorite color may be red. That is my perception. But whether or not a color is in fact red is reality.

A color-blind person certainly struggles with perception and reality. That's why we need an objective reference point. I am not good with differentiating colors. The other day after a funeral service I put down my jacket where a few others had also been taken off and left. When it was time to leave, I went back to the pile and picked up a jacket. A blue one fit me quite well, but I returned it to the pile because I had lost a black one. You guessed it: after a long search I tried the "blue" jacket again and, behold, it was mine!

Louise tells me that I wrongly perceive color quite often. The problem is that my perception is not reality. There is a standard of correctness when it comes to color. Even if I cannot perceive it, my lack of perception does not alter the truth.

So who decides what is right and what is wrong? Western society seems less inclined toward the Bible, preferring views like:

- "It's right as long as it doesn't hurt anybody else."
- "It's right because everyone else is doing it too."
- "It's right if you feel like it is right."
- "There is no such thing as right and wrong anymore."

If there is no basis for right and wrong, then why do we still claim that it is wrong to maim or to murder? If everything is permitted as long as we feel like it, then why do we have any laws? Can you imagine the chaos that would result if we simply told everyone, "There is no right and wrong. You can do whatever you like"? The truth is, we are already seeing some of those consequences. We live increasingly in an amoral society—and we are seeing the disastrous results.

THE CALL TO HOLY LIVING

The Bible reveals that God is holy, and we are called to holy living (1 Peter 1:16). God's unchanging Word is the basis for that holiness. If we simply make up our own moral code and then redefine it every few years based on popular opinion, then what kind of standard of right and wrong would that be?

A foundational Bible passage on the subject of holy living is Deuteronomy 6:1–7. In this passage, Moses addressed the nation of Israel before they entered the Promised Land:

> These are the commands, decrees and laws the LORD your God directed me to teach you to observe in the land that you are crossing the Jordan to possess, so that you, your children and their children after them may fear the LORD your God as long as you live by keeping all his decrees and commands that I give you, and so that you may enjoy long life. Hear, Israel, and be careful to obey so that it may go well with you and that you may increase greatly in a land flowing with milk and honey, just as the LORD, the God of your ancestors, promised you.
>
> Hear, O Israel: The LORD our God, the LORD is one. Love the LORD your God with all your heart and with all your soul and with all your strength. These commandments that I give you today are to be on your hearts. Impress them on your children. Talk about them when you sit at home and when you walk along the road, when you lie down and when you get up.

The Bible commands parents to lovingly teach their children about "the commands, decrees and laws" of God (v. 1). A child's first duty is to obey his or her parents (Ephesians 6:1; Colossians 3:20). But children must also grow to be responsible, to respect their parents, and above all to respect the Lord. Then it will be their generation's turn to repeat the pattern for teaching their children the commands and laws of God, bearing in mind that only a true heart knowledge of God's laws (and not mere head knowledge) will endure.

If there is no right and wrong, then there is nothing to obey, no commandment, no need of any rebuke or correction, no admonishment, no coaching, and no need to teach goodness. The argument shifts at this point to "there is no good" or to the more fantastic view that "we are all good." Obviously this view doesn't come from parents of young children or from observable science! This is merely the popular opinion of the day, when people justify their behaviors by saying, "We can do whatever we like."

TODDLER TANTRUM

Recently Louise and I witnessed a toddler tantrum in a grocery store. This little one was throwing himself around and wailing loudly. Poor parents! As they say in the South, "Bless their hearts." (Honestly, it is best not to judge anyone when you come across a similar situation because many of us have been in the place of that parent and child. And don't take a video and post it on YouTube!)

What do we call children who have no discipline? We say they are *spoiled*, which means "ruined."

If we want to avoid ruin, we must embrace the need for discipline according to a standard. Success occurs when we rarely do what we want to do and mainly do what we must do. If it is time for work, you could say, "I want to fish." But that is not helpful. It's time for work. So get up, show up, and you can fish afterward. Delayed gratification and self-discipline are in conflict with today's ethic that says, "We want it all and want it now."

Our Western heritage, now under fire, once had a general confidence in God's existence and the absolute truth of certain Christian standards. No one but Jesus Christ ever lived perfectly, of course. But there is a right and wrong. God has given us a standard.

WHAT STANDARD?

Growing up, most of us used in our school classrooms a wonderful contraption: a wooden ruler. A foot is twelve inches. Not eleven or fifteen. There is a standard.

We hear today that all standards are to be rejected as old-fashioned and no longer relevant. But what standard has replaced the old standards? Now, I am not saying we need to go back in time. Every era has its blind spots and sins. But today's popular viewpoint of rejecting absolute truth can be expressed something like this:

"Your God is dead, but my godlessness is enlightened and you have to be tolerant of me. You must absolutely never claim absolute truth or a moral standard. Your different view is intolerant, and you are therefore not to be tolerated. If you disagree with my view, then you are intolerant and must be silenced. You deserve to lose your job for daring to believe the old things. Forget freedom of speech (which they tell us in the American citizenship test is a very important right, and why the founders came here in the first place). If you use your speech to speak against what I believe, then you are bad. It is acceptable for you to lose your job or freedom and suffer economic hardships for making me feel bad. Making me feel bad (even if you didn't intend it) by declaring a standard of morality is intolerable. After all, we all evolved from random chance, so there is no God to tell us what to do. The old ethics are intolerant and irrelevant. My view is the fittest, and my view can condemn you to history. Your time is over. We can now do whatever we like."

This viewpoint isn't new. Neither are the logical consequences of it. The author of the book of Judges declared, "In those days Israel had no king; everyone did as they saw fit" (21:25).

What are the dangers of living without a standard of right and wrong?

THE CONSEQUENCES OF
NO RIGHT AND WRONG

Let's consider the logical consequences of this idea that there is no longer any definitive standard of right and wrong. What kind of a world would we live in if it were okay to steal, drive however fast we want to, or eat a whole package of Oreos without offering one to anyone else? The issue goes back to who decides what the standard of right and wrong is.

Benjamin Rush, one of America's founding fathers, suggested that the order of priorities for believers should be God, country, family. Rush believed that the prevailing culture mattered and that there needed to be a basis of right. If we lose the country, we will eventually lose the family. When we lose our sense of right and wrong on the inside, then we will lose all restraint and order on the outside.

During our tour of Washington, D.C., Louise and I went to the Lincoln Memorial with our friends Dr. John and Donna Avant. I read the Gettysburg Address inscribed on one side while John read the Second Inaugural Address on the other. Then John suggested that I read the address, saying, "This was a theological treatise." In the United States of America, God was once understood to be an integral part of governance and right living.

There is no sense of good and bad without God. There is no need for parental guidance if the kids are free to make their own choices. There is no need for parents to teach their children right from wrong when the kids can do whatever they want. In fact, there may eventually not even be a need for parents to raise children at all. Marriage and family values are old-fashioned, people say. If we sit idly by, we will be amazed by how all traces of God can be eliminated from our culture. However, God's truth will prevail. As believers, we need to stand up and proclaim that truth, regardless of the dominant beliefs in the present culture. And we know that God ultimately will reveal His authority to the world.

GOD HAS SPOKEN

In contrast to the prevailing worldview, Christians believe that God has spoken—and He has spoken to us in His Word, the Bible.

In Exodus 20:3–17, God revealed the Ten Commandments to His people. Here is a summary of those ten key biblical principles:

1. You shall have no other gods before Me.
2. You shall not make idols.
3. You shall not take the name of the Lord your God in vain.
4. Remember the Sabbath day, to keep it holy.
5. Honor your father and your mother.
6. You shall not murder.
7. You shall not commit adultery.
8. You shall not steal.
9. You shall not bear false witness against your neighbor.
10. You shall not covet.

This is God's revealed standard of righteousness to live by.

When Jesus came, He said, "Do not think that I have come to abolish the Law or the Prophets; I have not come to abolish them but to fulfill them" (Matthew 5:17). This means that Jesus did not dumb down God's requirements. Instead, He came to give us the grace and power we need to fulfill the righteous requirements of the law in Him.

Jesus submitted to the law. The law convicts us of sin and shows us our need for the Savior. The Sermon on the Mount takes us to the heart of revealed and enduring truth. Jesus said,

> You have heard that it was said to the people long ago, "You shall not murder, and anyone who murders will be subject to judgment." But I tell you that anyone who is angry with a brother or sister will be

subject to judgment. Again, anyone who says to a brother or sister, "Raca," is answerable to the court. And anyone who says, "You fool!" will be in danger of the fire of hell. (Matthew 5:21–22)

The Old Testament is clear. Murder is wrong.

"Ah, that is so Old Testament," some say. "The New Testament will be softer, surely."

But when Jesus came, He didn't abolish this command. Instead, He took it to the next level. Jesus taught that not only is murder wrong, but anger and hatred are wrong too. We are not to get enraged at someone or call him or her names. You may say, "I have never committed murder," but you can still be a selfish person or a lousy friend and therefore break this commandment.

Then Jesus Christ, who fulfilled the law, went beyond the law to the heart of reconciliation and healing:

Therefore, if you are offering your gift at the altar and there remember that your brother or sister has something against you, leave your gift there in front of the altar. First go and be reconciled to them; then come and offer your gift. (vv. 23–24)

Next, Jesus addressed the subject of right and wrong in regard to sexual ethics. He began by quoting the Old Testament commandment:

You have heard that it was said, "You shall not commit adultery." (5:27)

That was the Old Testament law—sex outside of marriage was forbidden. But surely the New Testament would be softer and easier? The newest writing would have evolved to be easier and nicer, right? Let's look at what Jesus taught:

> But I tell you that anyone who looks at a woman lustfully has already committed adultery with her in his heart. (5:28)

Jesus again went to the very heart of the matter, to our deepest motives. He taught that we should not commit adultery, and we should not have a desire for it either. It is not okay just to say, "I have never committed adultery." Sex is about covenant relationship and faithfulness. You can avoid technical adultery yet still have a pornographic mind. You may avoid having sex with someone you are not married to, but it is also sinful to watch other people committing adultery or having orgies online.

Then Jesus addressed the number one issue of impurity: lust. He stated with absolute clarity what marriage is and rejected the Pharisees' attempts to downgrade the sacredness of marriage. Jesus reaffirmed that marriage is between one man and one woman (Matthew 19:5), confirming the holiness of this Old Testament standard. Those who say that Jesus never addressed the issue of marriage reveal that they are not in the least bit interested in what He actually and clearly said. If you don't like what Jesus said about marriage being only between a man and a woman, at least be honest about it. You can reject Him, but don't twist His words.

The Bible is God's revelation. He has clearly established

His standard of right and wrong. He has a right to declare it, for He made us and He is righteous. He only commands what is good. He wants us to have joy.

Right and wrong are based on God's unchanging revelation, not people's ever-changing opinions. There is a standard of right and wrong; it comes from the God of the Bible. Deny this, and it is as if the telescope is broken or has dropped into the ocean.

JESUS HELPS US UPHOLD GOD'S STANDARD

A cocky young man, sometimes called the rich young ruler, once boasted to Jesus that he had kept the entire law of God all by himself.

> A man came up to Jesus and asked, "Teacher, what good thing must I do to get eternal life?"
>
> "Why do you ask me about what is good?" Jesus replied. "There is only One who is good. If you want to enter life, keep the commandments."
>
> "Which ones?" he inquired.
>
> Jesus replied, "'You shall not murder, you shall not commit adultery, you shall not steal, you shall not give false testimony, honor your father and mother,' and 'love your neighbor as yourself.'"
>
> "All these I have kept," the young man said. "What do I still lack?" (Matthew 19:16–20)

Really? This man was bragging that he had kept every single one of God's laws perfectly?

Believing in right and wrong should not make us proud but humble. We should understand that we have sinned and ask God for His grace. God is perfectly righteous and holy. We are not. We need help, so God has sent help. Jesus is the Savior, the Lamb of God whose sacrifice covered over all our sins. As our sacrificial Lamb, Jesus fulfills the Old Testament requirements as both the suffering sacrifice and the victorious Messiah.

Jesus was sacrificed on the cross on our behalf, so that no animal needed to be sacrificed again. The Bible calls each of us to humbly admit, "It is I who have sinned." Each one of us has sinned and fallen short of God's perfect standard of right and wrong (Romans 3:23).

God the Father sent His Son to put His law on our hearts and minds—to give us the gift of righteousness where we were wrong. Loving fathers do this.

Jesus was sacrificed in our place. The righteous Son of God was slain not for the righteous but the undeserving (2 Corinthians 5:21). And Romans 8:1 tells us that the result of Jesus's sacrifice is there is no longer any condemnation from God for those who trust Christ.

DO WE STILL HAVE TO OBEY?

Some Christians ask, "Now that we have Jesus, we don't have to obey God's laws anymore, right? Since we now live by grace, can't we just forget all those older scriptures and commands?"

It is true that Jesus Christ is the sacrificial Lamb whose death covered over all our sins. In Him the Old Testament

Law is fulfilled. Yes, we are saved by grace and we live by grace.

But we still obey.

Matthew 28:19–20 reminds us to declare the gospel but also to make disciples, which means to teach others to do God's will. We teach them to obey God. In this passage, Jesus gave this command to His followers:

> Therefore go and make disciples of all nations, baptizing them in the name of the Father and of the Son and of the Holy Spirit, and teaching them to obey everything I have commanded you. And surely I am with you always, to the very end of the age.

The apostle Paul also confirmed the ongoing need for Christ-followers to obey God's laws in this series of verses that he penned in the fifth chapter of his letter to the Galatians:

> It is for freedom that Christ has set us free. Stand firm, then, and do not let yourselves be burdened again by a yoke of slavery. (v. 1)

> You were running a good race. Who cut in on you to keep you from obeying the truth? (v. 7)

> You, my brothers and sisters, were called to be free. But do not use your freedom to indulge the flesh;

rather, serve one another humbly in love. For the entire law is fulfilled in keeping this one command: "Love your neighbor as yourself." (vv. 13–14)

So I say, walk by the Spirit, and you will not gratify the desires of the flesh. (v. 16)

The acts of the flesh are obvious: sexual immorality, impurity and debauchery; idolatry and witchcraft; hatred, discord, jealousy, fits of rage, selfish ambition, dissensions, factions and envy; drunkenness, orgies, and the like. I warn you, as I did before, that those who live like this will not inherit the kingdom of God.

But the fruit of the Spirit is love, joy, peace, forbearance, kindness, goodness, faithfulness, gentleness and self-control. Against such things there is no law. Those who belong to Christ Jesus have crucified the flesh with its passions and desires. Since we live by the Spirit, let us keep in step with the Spirit. (vv. 19–25)

Notice that Paul described the new life in Christ as one that is characterized by "love, joy, peace, forbearance, kindness, goodness, gentleness and self-control" (vv. 22–23). Our freedom in Christ does not mean that we are free to do anything we want to. It means we are free to do everything God wants us to.

TOO NARROW?

While visiting London in 2016, I spoke to a Korean student who had once been a church attender. She said she had left after finding church too "narrow." I tried to find out if the church was just culturally limited or if she was resisting the call of God to obey Him. When we don't want to do God's will, we declare that it is narrow! But undoubtedly some churches can become restrictive in a way that doesn't make us good or righteous.

I shared that Jesus said, "The truth will set you free" (John 8:32). Jesus calls us to get off the broad way that leads to death and get on the narrow way that leads to life (Matthew 7:13). Just because I feel His pull or push to obey Him and just because God's will may be difficult or counter-intuitive does not make it wrong. It is better.

So many have concluded that there is no right or wrong and no rhyme or reason for existence. All codes of good conduct are societal constructs that restrict us. But many cultures have tried throwing off all restraint and it has been a disaster. The Bible gives historical accounts of several examples of this. I would suggest that the fall of the Roman Empire is a good example. I pray that a study of Britain or America will not someday be the story of Rome.

The very fact that we can reason and reject right and wrong is surely proof that our existence matters. If it doesn't matter, then why do some people get so heated arguing with those who do believe in right and wrong? Those denying any moral code do seem to get very "moral" about it.

You only have one life. So be on the side of doing right

even if that means walking the narrow way, which, by the way, Jesus said leads to life. That sounds much better than death!

We need to do our own reflection here. Does it make sense to have no point whatsoever to life and no ethical basis for anything in life? It may just be that those who view morality through the telescope of a revealed belief have helped keep much of this world from self-destruction.

THE HUNDRED-YEAR EXPERIMENT

I preached in Wales during the one hundredth anniversary of the Great War (1914–18). This was a terrible war. About nine hundred thousand British men were killed in the trenches of Belgium and France. Recently, the same number of ceramic poppies created one of the greatest wonders of modern art surrounding the Tower of London. In the face of so many deaths, during the war a wave of grief went over the nation as well as many other nations. Two of my great-grandfather's brothers were killed in that war. My great-grandfather went to the front lines, to certain injury or death. The day before he was due to enter combat peace was declared, saving his life.

But the nation was affected. It was around this time when church attendance in Britain began to decline. We were suffering from national shock and sorrow, and many were disillusioned with life.

So for about one hundred years, Britain drifted from God. Church attendance withered, and churches seemed dull and lifeless. God was left out more and more.

I asked several groups in Britain in 2014, "What are the results of this decline in church attendance? Is life now better or worse? Is society more loving and kind? Are addictions up or down? How did that work for us the last hundred years?"

Those in the audience knew the answer: our hundred-year rejection of God had failed. So I proposed a suggestion: Why don't we try the alternative? The status quo was to reject God, and we were experiencing the negative consequences of that choice. Why not break the hundred-year curse and turn back to God?

One day I gave this message at a rugby club of which I am member. There were almost no churchgoers in attendance, but almost all of those who were present responded to the message and acknowledged Jesus as Lord!

Maybe you need to do that yourself right now. Agree that God is holy. Confess that you have sinned. Believe in Jesus, who fulfilled God's righteousness on your behalf through His cross and resurrection. Receive His Holy Spirit, who will give you the fruit of a new life.

There is no better foundation. Now we are on our way to seeing farther through our imaginary telescope.

IS THE BIBLE
RELIABLE?

After Louise and I finished our lunch at a local restaurant one day, I invited our waiter to come to our church. He appeared to be mildly interested but said, "Surely the Bible is so old that it must be full of mistakes. Time passing must have distorted the original."

Just like that, we had arrived at the third of the seven great questions: Is the Bible reliable?

I mentioned to the waiter that I was writing this very chapter. In a few moments I summarized for him a few of the thoughts that I will share in these pages.

"Very helpful," he said, seeming to be truly surprised by how much evidence to support the veracity of the Bible.

IS THE BIBLE FULL OF FAIRY TALES?

You may have heard people say, "The Bible is full of fairy tales." Actually, there are no fairy tales in the Bible whatsoever.

None at all. No fairies. If fact, the next time someone claims there are fairy tales in the Bible, ask them to give you an example.

Is the Bible full of fairy tales that have been disproven by science and history? It is stunning how some people are 100 percent resolved against the Bible, based on completely erroneous assumptions. Others like myself believe quite the opposite.

The Bible includes historical narratives, stories, parables, laws, songs, proverbs, and apocalyptic literature. It contains some of the greatest and most beloved stories of all time. It chronicles the lives of historically recognized figures like Abraham, Nehemiah, Daniel, Nebuchadnezzar, John the Baptist, and, arguably, the most influential person in history: Jesus of Nazareth. This is not a book of mythical figures or fairy tales. No serious scholar doubts the existence of these history makers, many of whom are named in records outside the Bible as well as within it. These are well-recognized, respected real people written about by prominent, historical authors.

Nothing has guided me more clearly, convicted me more painfully, or encouraged me more deeply than God's Word. The apostle Paul wrote,

> But as for you, continue in what you have learned and have become convinced of, because you know those from whom you learned it, and how from infancy you have known the Holy Scriptures, which are able to make you wise for salvation through faith

in Christ Jesus. All Scripture is God-breathed and is useful for teaching, rebuking, correcting and training in righteousness, so that the servant of God may be thoroughly equipped for every good work. (2 Timothy 3:14–17)

The aim of this chapter is for us to become more certain of the reliability of the Bible. This is a vital third section of our extending telescope. We will look at some facts that I hope lead all of us to more than just head knowledge but to a deeper desire to read, remember, and realize the Word daily and constantly in our lives.

WHO WROTE THE BIBLE?

The Bible is made up of sixty-six books, written by forty authors in three languages on three continents over fifteen hundred years. Most holy books have only one author. Remarkably, the fact that the Bible has so many authors and witnesses adds strength to the Bible's reliability. But ultimately, the Bible is divinely inspired. The Bible was a team effort, and its power is divine.

The Bible claims that, through divine inspiration, credible human authors wrote intelligently in or from their life contexts. The apostle Peter explained,

Above all, you must understand that no prophecy of Scripture came about by the prophet's own interpretation of things. For prophecy never had its origin in the human will, but prophets, though

human, spoke from God as they were carried along
by the Holy Spirit. (2 Peter 1:20–21)

Some of the biblical writers are relatively unknown, but
most are well-documented figures such as Moses, David,
Solomon, Luke, Peter, and Paul.

Even though many hands wrote down the words of the
Bible over many years, the story gloriously complements itself from beginning to end. Bible scholars call this "internal
consistency." Each book of the Bible brings a unique contri-
bution. Together, they all make sense.

A good example of this concept are the four Gospels in
the New Testament: Matthew, Mark, Luke, and John. Each
has a different author, yet together they present a complete
picture of Jesus's life on earth.

The Bible came together across so many years and
through so many pens because, above all, it has one divine
Author. That is what makes the Bible unique.

IS THE BIBLE HISTORICALLY ACCURATE?

Among other things, the Old Testament is a book of history.
The British have the Domesday Book. The French have the
Bayeux Tapestry. The Egyptians have their hieroglyphics,
and Americans have the Declaration of Independence and
the Constitution. These writings and depictions are not
only historical, but they are also prime sources of history
itself.

The Old Testament presents the history of Israel. The
Israelites understood the importance of preserving their

history and the laws. Scripture describes how the priests carried the Ten Commandments on two tablets of stone contained within the ark of the covenant in order to protect this first written record from the hand of God.

If you want history, read the Old Testament. The events really happened. If the stories told in Scripture were myth, they would not have endured in the life of a nation as its core story. Myth histories have a recognizable fictional flair and obvious lack of historicity. Not so with the Old Testament. If you want to know what happened, read the Bible. This is also a book that can tell you why things happened.

Nineteenth-century liberal theologians—who were doubting or disbelieving scholars—suggested that the Bible was more myth than truth. How do we know that any of this even took place?

Some of the attacks challenged even the most basic history. For instance, they asked, was there a wall in Jericho? (And if so, did God knock it down?) Answer. Yes. You can visit Jericho today. The wall fell in such a way that was unusual, not what you would expect in a siege.[1]

The critics also were certain that King David and King Hezekiah didn't even exist. Myths tend not to be about real people or places. It is all fantasy. Well, in recent years we are seeing that these attacks were unfounded because evidence is emerging to reinforce the history given in the Bible.

And now the facts are increasingly strengthening. The CNN website reported a discovery announced across the world in 2015: "A dump site is the last place you would expect to find an 8th century B.C. seal for a papyrus document signed by one of the kings of Judah. Perhaps that's why it has taken 2,700 years for the piece of clay inscribed with King Hezekiah's seal to be discovered in Jerusalem. It is believed to be the first-ever seal, or 'bulla,' from an Israeli or Judean King to be discovered by archaeologists.

"The seal of the king was so important. It could have been a matter of life or death, so it's hard to believe that anyone else had the permission to use the seal," Eilat Mazar, who directs excavations at the City of David's summit, told CNN. "Therefore, it's very reasonable to assume we are talking about an impression made by the King himself, using his own ring."[2]

Each year *Christianity Today* reveals the top ten biblical discoveries of the year. In their article "Biblical Archaeology's Top Ten Discoveries of 2015," the enthralling Hezekiah seal is only number three![3] The point is that each year that goes by reveals more, not less, of the Bible as history.

Of course, archeology alone does not prove that the Bible is the inspired Word of God, but it does prove that it is not myth and that the Bible stories and characters are real.

The New Testament is also a book of real history. Like the Old Testament, the New Testament Scriptures were carefully preserved. The persecutions of Christians after AD 30 created an imminent, intense need to protect the Scriptures, and this made the Bible's preservation more certain. Within fifty years of Jesus's resurrection, the vast majority of the New Testament was written. The sheer volume of texts points to the high value that believers placed on the Scriptures.

WHAT ABOUT THE OTHER GOSPELS?

When other writings appeared—heresies and false Gospels, they were not accepted into the New Testament because they were not credible. The councils of Nicea and Chalcedon in the fourth century addressed the issue of the so-called Gnostic Gospels. They met to determine what the true books of the Bible's canon or collection were. The more they studied, the more it became clear that the four Gospels (Matthew, Mark, Luke, and John) were far superior and more authentic than the newer, Gnostic Gospels.

The Gospels deemed to be authentic were authored by true eyewitnesses. The rejected Gospels had no historical chain connecting the author to Jesus or to a known eyewitness of Jesus's life. The texts that do have a historical chain consistently present a uniform picture of a Jesus who never sinned.

The Gospel of Thomas (one of the rejected Gospels) was used as the lead source in the fictional book *The Da Vinci Code*.[4] The thesis of the novel (though *thesis* is a strong word, as it is just a gripping yarn) holds up the false Gospel of Thomas as a paragon of feminist liberation. The novel's author, Dan Brown, claims that is why the church rejected it and why Thomas's Gospel is not in our Bibles. But when we actually read the Gospel of Thomas, we find the exact opposite. It contains a bizarre, anti-woman phrase, with Jesus supposedly saying that "every woman who makes herself male will enter the kingdom of heaven."[5] In other words, the Gospel of Thomas says that a woman must become a man in order to enter the kingdom of God. That is perhaps the most anti-female statement there could be!

Early Christian councils recognized that in order for a letter or Gospel to be accepted into the Bible, the writers of New Testament Scripture needed to have witnessed the risen Lord. Their descriptions needed apostolic authenticity. By the third century, official church councils came together to discern which so-called Gospel books were valid. Just as *The Da Vinci Code* was imaginatively written but laughably inaccurate with no credible source material, these false Gospels were obviously invalid and belonged in the fiction section. Only the original four Gospels—Matthew, Mark, Luke, and John—were found to be true. So the councils voted the fake and weird "Gospels" off the island.

The Bible is always in the nonfiction section. It is gospel truth.

HOW MUCH TIME ELAPSED BETWEEN THE EVENTS AND THE NEW TESTAMENT ACCOUNTS?

People have often stated to me as if it were fact, "Rhys, there is such a long gap between the events and the writing that the essential truth of the Bible has been twisted. So much time elapsed between the event and the record of Scripture that it could have all been changed." But the facts about the Bible reveal the opposite. The historical and literary evidence for the short time between the events and the writing is a great strength for the reliability of Scripture.

One of the best examples of this is the Bible book of 1 Corinthians. The apostle Paul wrote this letter to the church in Corinth just twenty years after the events he described took place. Just twenty years. Myth-development theory suggests that mythical claims tend to get bolder as the time gap increases, especially as eyewitnesses to an event have died and no one is around to refute any untruths or exaggerations. Yet this early letter from Paul contains the boldest of all the claims of the resurrection of Jesus. The apostle Paul recorded that Jesus rose, appeared on many separate occasions, and then appeared to more than five hundred witnesses, most of whom were still alive.

> For what I received I passed on to you as of first im-
> portance: that Christ died for our sins according to
> the Scriptures, that he was buried, that he was raised
> on the third day according to the Scriptures, and
> that he appeared to Cephas, and then to the Twelve.
> After that, he appeared to more than five hundred
> of the brothers and sisters at the same time, most
> of whom are still living, though some have fallen
> asleep. Then he appeared to James, then to all the
> apostles, and last of all he appeared to me also, as to
> one abnormally born. (1 Corinthians 15:3–8)

This text was written within twenty years of the events, and it was written in such a fashion that many suggest its core truths had been recounted and memorized very accurately as oral tradition within five years of the events. The fact that Paul stated most of these eyewitnesses were still living meant that they therefore could be cross-examined.

Some say that a significant gap passed between the event

of the resurrection and the writing of the Gospels, and this could have led to the story being exaggerated. I say that the experience of losing a loved one is as vivid a moment as one could ever recall. My father died in 1978, and more than thirty years after that event, I still clearly remember many details of his last days. I can see the blue light of the police car arriving at our house. I can hear the rain falling and recall the feeling of a sense that something was wrong. Then came the news, and the next days are as vivid now as they were thirty-seven years ago.

The story of the resurrection was in written form well within this length of time. To say that a twenty-year gap between such vital events and the recording of them would have led to gross exaggeration by all witnesses involved is not credible.

Nor does this claim do justice to the reliability of local and eyewitness accounts in a time when history was carefully passed down through oral tradition. As Paul said in 1 Corinthians 15:3, "For what I received I passed on to you."

At the heart of this material are the death and resurrection of Jesus. Almost certainly Paul's words mean that the events of Jesus's life were already being written, remembered, and recounted at the time he wrote this letter to the Corinthians. Even within that short period of time, the essential story of Jesus was already being preserved in oral tradition.

This is solid historical and literary proof that there is virtually no gap between the events and the writing of the New Testament. The cynic may make it sound as if the Bible were buried for centuries, randomly found, and then fictionalized—but this is not the case.

ARE THE COPIES OF THE BIBLE ACCURATE?

Recent archaeological discoveries have proven to be a great boost for the reliability of Bible history and Bible facts.

Codex Sinaiticus

In 1844, Count Tischendorf, a Bible scholar, discovered the Codex Sinaiticus manuscript at the St. Catherine Monastery at Mount Sinai. It was the world's oldest and most complete Bible, dating from AD 325, and now resides in the British Library in London and as a digitalized version on the Internet.[6] This is one example of many very old copies of Scripture.

Dead Sea Scrolls Found at Qumran

The day before the creation of the state of Israel in 1948, a miracle occurred: the Dead Sea Scrolls were found.

When I visited Qumran with a team from our church in 2010, I was very encouraged. These scrolls, including some of the oldest copies of the Old Testament, are further proof that living communities had preserved the Scriptures in painstaking fashion.

The large body of early copies of Scripture has increased, not decreased.

Painstaking Preservation

When people developed the ability to write on papyrus, this greatly helped the writing and preservation of the Bible. Luke 4 tells us that Jesus unrolled Scripture scrolls in the synagogue:

He went to Nazareth, where he had been brought up, and on the Sabbath day he went into the synagogue, as was his custom. He stood up to read, and the scroll of the prophet Isaiah was handed to him. Unrolling it, he found the place where it is written:

"The Spirit of the Lord is on me,
  because he has anointed me
  to proclaim good news to the poor.
He has sent me to proclaim freedom for the prisoners
    and recovery of sight for the blind,
to set the oppressed free,
  to proclaim the year of the Lord's favor."

Then he rolled up the scroll, gave it back to the attendant and sat down. The eyes of everyone in the synagogue were fastened on him. He began by saying to them, "Today this scripture is fulfilled in your hearing." (vv. 16–21)

We can observe from the careful way Jesus treated the scroll in the synagogue that during the time of the New Testament, the Old Testament was lovingly and skillfully preserved, protected, and read.

The Bible was carefully kept by the nation of Israel and later by the followers of Jesus. The advent of printing was timed perfectly for the propagation of the Bible. The God of the Bible still does Bible-like things. As the gospel began to spread throughout Europe and Asia along Roman roads, so the invention of the printing press sped the global availability of the Bible.

The Gutenberg Bible was printed in 1455. The next century, William Tyndale translated the Bible into English, drawing from the original Greek and Hebrew rather than the Latin translation, all the while praying for God to change the heart of the king of England toward allowing a Bible in the common language. Though he was burned at the stake for his efforts, Tyndale's magnificent courage led to the first official Authorized Version of the Bible, available to the common person.

The Bible has continued to spread throughout the world. Now we have dozens of translations, copies of the Bible available in every bookstore, and even Bible apps for our smartphones. The Internet now provides the means for a free and widely accessible Bible.

The Bible is the most carefully written, replicated, and protected of all texts. While the huge number of well-preserved Bibles and the accuracy of the many copies of the Bible do not in themselves prove that the Bible we have is the inspired Word of God, they do prove that the Bible we have is the same Bible that was used in antiquity.

The Bible has influenced culture and shaped history, bringing freedom to many people and creating more schools, hospitals, universities, and orphanages than any other book, philosophy, or religion. The Bible is the greatest liberator, so attacks on the Bible and Bible people are the greatest threats to freedom.

IS IT ALL A HOAX?

What about modern discoveries in the field of archaeology? Hasn't science proven the Bible to be all wrong? This reminds me of a neighbor in Brighton, England, who said to me one day in his Scottish accent, quite matter-of-factly, "Of course science has disproven the Bible!" Was he right?

Actually, the more discoveries that historians and archaeologists make about the ancient world, the more ground the skeptics lose. Let's look at eight facts about the reliability of your Bible.

1. Manuscript Reliability

No document in history has been as carefully preserved as the Bible. The number of biblical manuscripts we have is staggering, not to mention the references to a plethora of Bible verses in thousands of other writings.[7]

There are thousands more New Testament references in scores of other writings and sources in the second century. Be encouraged—the Bible is the most historically reliable of all sources.

2. Careful Preservation

In the days of oral tradition, large passages of foundational scriptures were put to song or rhyme. Philippians 2:6–11, for instance, shows evidence of this type of preservation, as do Colossians 1:15–20, often called the "Christ Hymn" by Bible commentators, and 1 Corinthians 15:3–8. Songs are very effective memory tools. Early believers learned Bible verses by song and repetition.

If you had the most important story of all and you were being persecuted, you could avoid detection by carefully remembering the details of the story and passing it on verbally. But as time passed, you would be keen to write it down. The evidence fits for the preservation and recording of the Bible.

A vast amount of Scripture has been copied throughout the past nineteen hundred years. Many Bibles have been kept for centuries. Mass printing has occurred for more than six hundred years. Pulpit Bibles have been lovingly preserved throughout the years since the New Testament. Countless people possess and cherish family Bibles, believing God's Word to be a worthy foundation for any home.

3. Historical Facts

Have you ever heard someone say, "The Bible is full of mistakes"? One of the biggest myths is that the Bible is a myth.

We can gain much from patiently spending a couple of minutes comparing two biblical texts. For example, consider the historical account of a siege recorded in 2 Kings 18:13–15:

> In the fourteenth year of King Hezekiah's reign, Sennacherib king of Assyria attacked all the fortified cities of Judah and captured them. So Hezekiah king of Judah sent this message to the king of Assyria at Lachish: "I have done wrong. Withdraw from me, and I will pay whatever you demand of me." The king of Assyria exacted from Hezekiah king of Judah three hundred talents of silver and thirty talents of gold. So Hezekiah gave him all the silver that was

found in the temple of the LORD and in the treasuries of the royal palace.

If you want to know what an ancient siege was like, read the Bible! We read of the intimidation of the experience and of the power and protection of the Lord. This is a true story. Not only is it in 2 Kings, but the same siege is also described in Isaiah 36. Many Bible stories do overlap. This is also part of the book's internal consistency.

But the truth of the Bible is backed up by other historical facts. Archaeologists have also found in Sennacherib's palace at Nineveh (modern-day Mosul in Iraq) exciting evidence of this siege, called Sennacherib's prism. This prism, a six-sided clay structure carved with Sennacherib's annals, is displayed in the British Museum. Read a portion of it here for yourself:

As for Hezekiah the Judahite, who did not submit to my yoke: forty-six of his strong, walled cities, as well as the small towns in their area, which were without number, by levelling with battering-rams and by bringing up seige-engines, and by attacking and storming on foot, by mines, tunnels, and breeches, I besieged and took them. . . . (Hezekiah) himself, like a caged bird I shut up in Jerusalem, his royal city. I threw up earthworks against him— . . . His cities, which I had despoiled, I cut off from his land, and to Mitinti, king of Ashdod, Padi, king of Ekron, and Silli-bêl, king of Gaza, I gave (them). And thus

I diminished his land. I added to the former tribute, and I laid upon him the surrender of their land
and imposts—gifts for my majesty. As for Hezekiah,
the terrifying splendor of my majesty overcame him,
and the Arabs and his mercenary troops which he
had brought in to strengthen Jerusalem, his royal
city, deserted him. . . . To pay tribute and to accept
servitude, he dispatched his messengers.[8]

The story concludes in the Bible, in 2 Kings 19:6–7:

Isaiah said to them, "Tell your master, 'This is what
the LORD says: Do not be afraid of what you have
heard—those words with which the underlings of
the king of Assyria have blasphemed me. Listen!
When he hears a certain report, I will make him
want to return to his own country, and there I will
have him cut down with the sword.'"

This last part, about Sennacherib's army being cut
down and denied their treasure, is what happened, though
Babylonian propaganda doesn't report this. There are plenty
of other corroborations of biblical texts with additional
historical facts. Many Bible place-names have been confirmed by archaeology, and many biblical locations are
still present today. Archaeologists have even found the
ruins of two of the towns that Jesus prophesied would be
destroyed—Chorazin and Bethsaida (Matthew 11:21).
You can seek out further historical and archeological

evidence for yourself. If you ever have the chance to visit Israel, take it! But if you are unable to travel to Israel, you can still go online and study Jerusalem. There you can zoom in on the Temple Mount, the Mount of Olives, Gethsemane, the House of Caiaphas, Nehemiah's wall, Hezekiah's tunnel, David's tomb, and the Pool of Bethesda. All of these are considered "grade A" sites. Guides in Israel suggest that grade A sites are as certain as we can be about an archeological site. The Temple Mount in Jerusalem is the area where Jesus was dedicated, ministered as a twelve-year-old, turned over the tables of the moneychangers the week before He was crucified, and where the curtain was torn in two when He died on the cross approximately half a mile away.

Outside of Jerusalem, you can also see Gideon's spring at Harod and the Sea of Galilee. In Nazareth, the synagogue is almost certainly the precise spot where Jesus worshiped for thirty years and read the Scripture as recorded in Luke 4. You can also go to Capernaum—called "Jesus Town" by locals—where Jesus lived for a time.

Visit Bethlehem from the shepherds' fields to the Church of the Nativity. Go to the Jordan River, and you will discover plenty more historical evidence of Joshua, John the Baptist, and Jesus. Real history occurred here. Even a visit to the Dead Sea helps you visualize the destruction of Sodom and Gomorrah and explains why the landscape is as it is.

There are a host of other archaeological digs that cor-roborate biblical records about places such as Bethsaida, Bethany, Caesarea Philippi, Capernaum, Cyprus, Galatia,

Philippi, Thessalonica, Berea, Athens, Corinth, Ephesus, Rome, Caesarea, and so on. The evidence of the Bible's reliability is widespread. The point is that archaeology proves further the historicity of the Bible.

4. Internal Consistency

The Bible is a magnificent tapestry. The more sections we open of the telescope, the more we see.

The Bible's central story is the redemption of mankind. After the glory of creation, mankind fell because of sin. The effects were devastating. Though God was offended by our sin, nonetheless He found a way to reconcile us to Himself.

It took a lamb.

We can see how the theme of redemption runs through Scripture through the blood sacrifice of a lamb.

In Genesis 22, God tested Abraham by calling for him to sacrifice his beloved son, Isaac. Then "Isaac spoke up and said to his father Abraham, 'Father?' 'Yes, my son?' Abraham replied. 'The fire and wood are here,' Isaac said, 'but where is the lamb for the burnt offering?' Abraham answered, 'God himself will provide the lamb for the burnt offering, my son.' And the two of them went on together" (vv. 7–8). Eventually the son was spared and a ram sacrificed in his place.

The question, "Where is the lamb?" is a central theme of the Bible. Is there a way we can be forgiven? Yes, though the blood of a lamb.

By the time of the exodus, during the plagues of God's judgment, the people were offered divine protection from condemnation though the sacrifice of a lamb. "Moses summoned all the elders of Israel and said to them, 'Go at once and select the animals for your families and slaughter the Passover lamb'" (Exodus 12:21). Those who obeyed and painted the blood of the lamb on their doorframes were spared from God's judgment.

In the Old Testament law, Israel was commanded to make various sacrificial offerings to remove sin. In one such offering, the priest "is to slaughter the lamb in the sanctuary area where the sin offering and the burnt offering are slaughtered" (Leviticus 14:13).

Though this animal sacrifice appeased God for a time, the need of the people was great. Israel fell to constant rebelliousness. A greater redemption was prophesied. So the "anointed one" or "the suffering servant" appeared in the teaching of the Old Testament prophets. Isaiah described the coming Messiah using the picture of the sacrificial lamb: "He was oppressed and afflicted, yet he did not open his mouth; he was led like a lamb to the slaughter, and as a sheep before its shearers is silent, so he did not open his mouth" (Isaiah 53:7). This is one of the prophecies that Jesus fulfilled. This time the beloved Son would not be spared but would freely give up His life.

So when John the Baptist saw Jesus for the first time in Jesus's earthly ministry, he exclaimed, "Look, the Lamb of God, who takes away the sin of the world!" (John 1:29).

It is unusual to call someone a lamb. But can you see how the story has been unfolding over centuries from the Bible? From Bible book to Bible book, and testament to testament,

Jesus had been revealed to be, in fact, the one and only Lamb of God, whose sacrificial death would take away the sins of the world.

Three years later, Jesus prepared to offer Himself as a sacrifice. "On the first day of the Festival of Unleavened Bread, when it was customary to sacrifice the Passover lamb, Jesus' disciples asked him, 'Where do you want us to go and make preparations for you to eat the Passover?'" (Mark 14:12). And then Jesus died on the cross as a sacrifice.

The apostle Paul described the crucifixion as the fulfillment of the Old Testament Passover: "For Christ, our Passover lamb, has been sacrificed" (1 Corinthians 5:7).

The Lord's Supper, also called Communion, focuses on Jesus's body and blood as the sacrifice that God accepted to pay the penalty for our sins.

Then, after His death, resurrection, and ascension, the Bible says that Jesus will return. The final picture of heaven and eternity includes the image of Jesus and a lamb. In his vision on the island of Patmos, the apostle John "saw a Lamb, looking as if it had been slain, standing at the center of the throne, encircled by the four living creatures and the elders" (Revelation 5:6). This is Jesus, the glorified Lamb!

In the new heaven and the new earth, the Lamb is the focus of our worship and service. John described it like this: "No longer will there be any curse. The throne of God and of the Lamb will be in the city, and his servants will serve him. They will see his face, and his name will be on their foreheads. There will be no more night. They will not need the light of a lamp or the light of the sun, for the Lord God

will give them light. And they will reign for ever and ever"
(Revelation 22:3–5).

So we see that the theme of the lamb runs through
centuries, from Genesis to Revelation. And what a theme
that is! The blood of Jesus, the Lamb of God, is for the
redemption and salvation of all who believe. The Bible
fits together like an extending telescope! The farther we
go, and the more sections we pull out, the more clearly we
see Him.

The Bible is the Word of God. It influences how we
think and its truths impact how we live. It contains the
greatest stories ever told, including the accounts of Noah,
Abraham, Moses, Elijah, Isaiah, Peter, Paul, and Jesus.
These stories of real people who endeavored to follow God
teach us and inspire us.

The Bible tells each story as it happened, and this means
not every story has a happy ending. Though the book of
Revelation assures us that believers will eventually have
a "happily ever after" in heaven, there are no fairy tales in
the pages of the Bible. The Bible's characters are messy.
Scripture doesn't hide the sins of famous kings like David
and Solomon, the betrayal by Judas, the denial of Peter, or
the doubts of Thomas.

In the New Testament we see Jesus's kindness, and the
stories read naturally and are consistent with His character, not bizarrely as in the fake Gospels. We have a righteous Savior, but also One who suffers, who was rejected
and despised.

The historical record in Acts of the New Testament

period following Jesus's resurrection finishes without a nice, neat bow on the ending. The final chapter of that book, Acts 28, leaves us wondering, *What happens next?* The Bible calls us to wrestle with a balance of truths. This makes it even more authentic.

The Bible is true to life. And it contains wisdom—the greatest words ever spoken.

5. *The Two Testaments*

I have had the conversation many times in Europe, some-times having been approached quite boldly, that the Bible is full of contradictions. Once, when I asked the other person to give me an example of these so-called contradictions, he replied, "'Too many cooks spoil the broth' contradicts 'Many hands make light work.'" Of course, neither of those state-ments is in the Bible. This goes to show that some people are skeptical of the Bible without having read and reflected on the actual words of Scripture. This explains why there are numerous testimonies about someone's perspective changing dramatically when he or she reads the Bible for the first time.

Other times people legitimately misunderstand how the truths of Scripture fit together. They may read an "eye for eye" in the Old Testament (Exodus 21:24) and "turn to them the other cheek" in the New Testament (Matthew 5:39) and think these statements are contradic-tory. In fact, these statements are not a contradiction at all. As the saying goes, "The Old Testament is the New Testa-ment concealed. The New Testament is the Old Testament revealed." Jesus Himself brought the two thoughts together in the Sermon on the Mount to explain how He fulfilled the deeper requirement of the Old Testament law through the New Covenant (Matthew 5:38–42).

There are no contradictions in the Bible. In fact, Scripture often ties together two or more truths in tension with one another. Like the strength of a suspension bridge, biblical truth is reinforced by this opposite pull held in support and balance.

6. Fulfilled Prophecies

The subject of fulfilled prophecies in the Bible could fill many books by itself. The Bible includes hundreds of prophecies about future events—most of which have already been fulfilled. Each fulfillment adds to the reliability of the Bible. In Christ's life alone, over three hundred prophecies were fulfilled, including:

- His virgin birth (Isaiah 7:14)
- His birth in Bethlehem (Micah 5:2)
- His escape to Egypt (Hosea 11:1)
- His ministry in Galilee (Isaiah 9:1–2)
- His triumphal donkey ride (Zechariah 9:9)
- His suffering and crucifixion (Psalm 69:21; 22:1, 16, 18; Isaiah 50:6; 53:7–12; Zechariah 12:10)
- His resurrection and ascension (Psalm 16:10; 49:15; 110:1)

Some skeptics say that Jesus was just a man who carefully orchestrated His days in order to act out the prophecies concerning the Messiah that He had read about in Scripture. However, there were events and circumstances that Jesus could not have manipulated, such as the place of His birth and things done to Him during His death, were He just a man and not also God.

Jesus said that His singular concern was obeying the Father (John 6:38). The cynic may claim that anyone could match a set of predictions, given the right circumstances. But Jesus fulfilled too many prophecies to credit it all to random chance. The odds against chance being the explanation go up with every prophecy fulfilled until they are astronomical and impossible to calculate.

And He is coming back! Jesus Himself predicted His return (Matthew 24:30–31). The Old Testament in one sense is one huge prophecy fulfilled primarily in the life of Jesus. His second coming will complete the remaining prophecies from the Old Testament as well as fulfilling those from the New Testament.

7. The Gospels and Jesus

There are four marvelous Gospels in the New Testament—Matthew, Mark, Luke, and John. I have read them many times, studied them in the original Greek, and preached through each Gospel over and over since my teens. These are the greatest works in history because in them we learn about the person of Jesus.

Jesus Christ is no fairy tale but a historical figure without compare, and His story is mentioned and confirmed in other historical writings of the time, including books by the ancient historians Josephus, Tacitus, and Pliny.

Four authors. Four Gospels. Four uniquely presented facets of Jesus's marvelous character, teaching, and miracles, as well as His crucifixion, burial, resurrection, ascension, enduring power through the Spirit, and second coming. These Gospels provide four opportunities to contradict and disprove the other Gospels, yet each corroborates the reliability of the others.

8. The Church Has Endured

Jesus spoke a promise in Caesarea Philippi that the gates of hell shall not prevail against the church (Matthew 16:18). After the death and resurrection of Jesus, the church—the followers of Jesus—multiplied and spread rapidly across the earth despite persecution. The authors of the New Testament and the leaders of the early church suffered martyrdom and exile for their faith. Miraculously, despite all that stands against the church even today, the promise of Jesus is and will remain true.

At the time of this writing, we are seeing a wave of persecution break out against Christians across the world. It is not the first time this has happened. It is a marvel that the church survived the brutal death of her Master along with all the apostles in the first half century of the church's life. In the early years of the church there were major persecutions led by the emperors Nero, Domitian, and Trajan. Every attempt to purify the church or cause a revival of the church has often been followed by attacks. Starting churches in new places has often led to martyrdom.

But Jesus promised about His church, "The gates of

Hades will not overcome it" (Matthew 16:18). The current attacks on the church are deeply disturbing and horrifying. Yet we must also believe that through these trials, the church will be purified. As is often the case, the seed will die, yet it will spring to life. Already stories are seeping out of good coming out despite persecution, even after the horrors done against the people of God.

The task of the church is still unfinished, but Jesus will return. I have experienced the same love among believers on different continents. The same Spirit of Christ is moving in great power still. Jesus Christ is every bit as alive and real as He ever was.

THE PERSON BEHIND THE BOOK

We know the Bible is reliable because Jesus is reliable. The Word can't be separated from the One who is the Word (John 1:1). Jesus is the One who said, "Everyone who hears these words of mine and puts them into practice is like a wise man who built his house on the rock" (Matthew 7:24). We cannot follow Jesus without His Word living in us. He is the rock. "These words of mine" are an inseparable part of a rock-solid life that will withstand the storms that will come.

In the Bible have the truth, the best seller, the Word of life (1 John 1:1). When we see the Bible, we see Jesus.

I was given a children's picture Bible when I was a baby. My mum often read the stories to me. I didn't understand the overall message of this book, but I knew that it was special. I often used to look at the picture of Jesus on the cross and ask, "Why did He die?" I did not understand the answer.

When I was fourteen, I heard the gospel in a few short sentences. I was told that I had sinned and that sinners couldn't enter heaven. That is the bad news. I finally understood that is why Jesus died. He took my place that I deserved on the cross. He took my sin upon Himself. All He asks is that I believe in Him to receive His forgiveness and a new birth. This is the good news! I asked Him to forgive me and to take up residence in my life. And He has!

I immediately started reading the Bible, beginning in the New Testament. I couldn't put it down. The Bible came alive to me in a new way. It spoke to me, to the church, and to the world. It still does.

Since then the Bible has been my foundation. Jesus said that the Word of God is the foundation of all of our lives (Matthew 7:24). And it works!

THE BIBLE HELPS IN TIMES OF TRAGEDY

Within a month of receiving Christ, I learned that my father had taken his life. Naturally, this event was shattering for us as a family. During that time, God's Word became more and not less real. The Bible is so real that there is much help it offers in all situations. There is no lack of struggle in the Scriptures. The cross and suffering are the very heart of the faith. Jesus is with us.

The Bible says of itself, "The law of the LORD is perfect, refreshing the soul" (Psalm 19:7). His Word gets me up in the morning. I start each day with the Bible. And the

Holy Spirit recalls His Word and reminds me of Scripture throughout the day. The Bible is "alive and active" (Hebrews 4:12). It is relevant to everything in our lives today.

THE BIBLE IS A RELIABLE GUIDE

The Bible is the Magna Carta, the Declaration of Independence, the Constitution of all literature. It is the best-selling book of all time, a global phenomenon. But more than that, it is life to every tribe and tongue. It is "a lamp for [our] feet, a light on [our] path" (Psalm 119:105). The Bible is good for each of us, especially during our trials and temptations.

The Word calls us to protect the life of the innocent, gives instructions for families, and guides nations and leaders. It tells us how to reconcile with our enemies and to live "peaceful and quiet lives in all godliness and holiness" (1 Timothy 2:2). The book of Daniel even tells about how Daniel and his friends ate a specific diet that brought extra physical health. The Word is good for the whole person.

Of course, there is nothing better for our spiritual health than being right with God. John 3:16 gives us eternal well-being: "For God so loved the world that he gave his one and only Son, that whoever believes in him shall not perish but have eternal life."

Living the way God calls us to live is not easy. But if we base our thoughts and actions on the Word of God, we will be like a house with a good foundation (Matthew 7:24). When we follow the ways outlined and taught in the Bible, we can have wisdom and even find life, both abundant and eternal.

The Bible is a book for all time. It may have been written years ago, but sin is the same. Man is the same. God is the same.

So far we have pulled out three sections of our extending telescope:

- God made the world.
- He has revealed right from wrong.
- The Bible is reliable.

We are starting to see more clearly.

I encourage you now to take God at His Word. It is far superior to the latest theories and fads; it will never let you down. The Bible is utterly reliable, so build your life on the rock-solid foundation of Scripture.

IS JESUS GOD?

One life stands above all. The most towering figure in history neither wielded a sword nor ran for office. When asked to lead an organization, He declined. Yet He is the greatest leader of all time. His influence touches me daily. He influences you even as you think about Him now.

He was such a figure that the apostle John—perhaps the closest eyewitness to His public life, the one who heard and saw and touched Him, who experienced the fullness of His presence on earth—described this figure as "the eternal life":

> That which was from the beginning, which we have heard, which we have seen with our eyes, which we have looked at and our hands have touched—this we proclaim concerning the Word of life. The life appeared; we have seen it and testify to it, and we proclaim to you the eternal life, which was with the Father and has appeared to us. We proclaim to

you what we have seen and heard, so that you also may have fellowship with us. And our fellowship is with the Father and with his Son, Jesus Christ. (1 John 1:1–3)

The truths you will learn in this chapter will remind you, reconnect you, or help you realize what this life is. The eternal life is Jesus Christ. When we find His life, then we can find our life—life as it should be and will be forever.

We have now come to our fourth great question: "Is Jesus God?" Let us fix our eyes on Jesus, as the book of Hebrews tells us to do (12:2). If the Son of God actually came from heaven to earth, then we would expect there to be something unique about Him. What kind of birth, behavior, choices, purpose, relationships, death, and after-effect would we expect from the One called "the Word of life" (1 John 1:1)?

HIS BIRTH

The Gospel of Matthew tells us that when Jesus came to earth as a baby, He was already a King. Now, when His Royal Highness Prince George was born to William and Kate in 2013, he was received with tremendous expectation and great fanfare across the world. Jesus, too, was exceptionally born.

At the time of Jesus's birth, there was great expectation for a coming Messiah. The Old Testament prophesied the birth of a Savior through a virgin seven centuries before it happened:

Therefore the Lord himself will give you a sign: The virgin will conceive and give birth to a son, and will call him Immanuel. (Isaiah 7:14)

The virgin birth was every bit as miraculous to the people of that era as it is to many of us who have grown up hearing the Christmas story. God alone could enable this miraculous birth. God the Son was born, and through Him God the Father would reconcile the world to Himself:

For God was pleased to have all his fullness dwell in [Jesus], and through him to reconcile to himself all things, whether things on earth or things in heaven, by making peace through his blood, shed on the cross. (Colossians 1:19–20)

If Jesus had been born through usual means—if conception and birth had happened for Him exactly as it did for you and me—then the Savior would be just a human, born from two human parents. If both of His parents were sinful humans, then Jesus would have inherited Adam's sin and been sinful like all of us who are descended from Adam. Thus He would have been in need of being saved Himself!

The apostle Paul affirmed the necessity of Jesus's virgin birth, which meant that Jesus did not inherit Adam's original sin. He wrote:

Sin entered the world through one man [Adam],

and death through sin, and in this way death came to all people, because all sinned—

Consequently, just as one trespass resulted in condemnation for all people, so also one righteous act resulted in justification and life for all people. For just as through the disobedience of the one man [Adam] the many were made sinners, so also through the obedience of the one man [Jesus] the many will be made righteous. (Romans 5:12, 18–19)

A sinful man cannot save another sinful man. Only a perfect, sinless God can save us. So Jesus was both God and man. Because He was born to a virgin, He did not inherit Adam's sin nature. In order to save us, Jesus had to be born as one of us, and He also had to be God.

THE TESTIMONY OF THE GOSPELS

Each of the four Gospels depicts the arrival of Jesus in some way, sometimes emphasizing the exceptional, sometimes the ordinary, but always that Jesus was the One and only God-man.

Matthew's Gospel is full of intrigue and fulfilled Scripture. The Romans ordered the people of Israel to go back to their hometowns to be counted for a census, a forced movement of the population emphasizing Rome's power and the poverty of the subdued nation. But the Romans did not write the larger narrative of the Grand Story. God arranged the Roman census. We see the angry, insecure King Herod in contrast to the righteous, willing, and diligent Mary and Joseph. Although the rulers of the Roman Empire might have overwhelmed the frail and humble people, ironically, the dominant powers were the ones most afraid.

Mathew gave us a list of the human ancestors of Jesus, proving His human credentials (Matthew 1:1–17). And then an angel appeared to Joseph in a dream and revealed the divine origin of this incarnation. The Child was from God. He had His plan all mapped out. The Magi saw it in the heavens—God was revealing Himself through His Son.

The Roman census of Matthew 2 sets Jesus in history— this was real life. Though Roman power seemed to reign, Christ was the true King. His kingdom would endure. It has endured and flourished long after Roman civilization was buried and dug up by archaeologists. The glorious kingdom of the Babe shall last forever.

The Gospel of Matthew repeatedly reminds us that Jesus's earthly ministry fulfilled the prophecies in the Old Testament that the Messiah would come with great effect but also to a little town called Bethlehem.

The Gospel of Mark is the shortest of the four Gospels, though it is still substantial. Mark emphasized the humility and service of the Messiah Jesus. He came not "to be served, but to serve, and to give his life as a ransom for many" (Mark 10:45). So Mark did not find it necessary to establish the kingly references concerning Jesus's birth, though all four Gospels affirm one another. Mark loved to tell how little fuss Jesus made of each miracle, caring for the one who received healing without wanting any publicity. How refreshing when today so many seem to worship the cult of celebrity. So we have Jesus beginning His ministry as a servant in the Gospel of Mark.

Luke's Gospel tells us more about Jesus's mother and human father. Luke wrote similarly to Matthew in that most of the details of Jesus's birth and the Christmas story come from these two Gospels. Luke told us much about Mary and Joseph and their cultural setting. Theirs was a regular Jewish home, and they faithfully observed the law of God. Luke is widely regarded as one of the greatest of all historians. The details matter, and his message about Jesus is clear:

> Today in the town of David a Savior has been born to you; he is the Messiah, the Lord. This will be a sign to you: You will find a baby wrapped in cloths and lying in a manger. (Luke 2:11–12)

The Gospel of John begins in heaven: "In the beginning was the Word, and the Word was with God, and the Word was God. He was with God in the beginning" (John 1:1–2). This is the true origin of Jesus. As all four Gospel writers show us, Jesus is the man from heaven. He is the Word— God made flesh. He came and pitched His tent among us, says John 1:14.

THE DIVINE CHRIST

One of the trends in some strands of theology is to separate Jesus from the church and say that after Jesus's resurrection and ascension, the church got carried away and created a fictitious Jesus they wanted, rather than the Jesus who actually was. This claim says that the biblical writers rewrote Jesus's story to change Him from being merely a good man into a man they imagined to be God. But this theory could not be further from the truth. Jesus was and is exactly who the Bible says He is.

All four Gospels begin with the divine origin of the Savior. They tell us of the One who is life—God in the flesh.

At the royal yet humble birth of Jesus, kings trembled, Magi searched, angels sang, and shepherds ran to Him. The only wise action was to seek Him and worship Him. The foolish reaction was to think of separating one's self from the family of Jesus, or of harboring jealousy and opposition toward Him. This theme follows Jesus throughout His life. He would be opposed. A sword pierced His mother's soul as she watched her son be crucified (Luke 2:35). He was destined to die for our sin. He is the Savior.

There simply is no other birth like His. So real yet humble; surprising yet long predicted; awaited and worthy of celebration. Your life and my life make sense only when we make Him our King.

JESUS'S EXTRAORDINARY LIFE

One Life stands above all others in history. It is an astonishing thing that though Jesus had no plane, car, or cell phone, though He never made a video, wrote a book, or Googled anything, He accomplished everything He set out to accomplish. His life has touched not only every continent over two thousand years but also every nation-state on earth. He ministered for just three years, and when He died He had few followers. Then He rose again. This changed everything. You and I can have no doubt that Jesus is unmatched.

What do we know of Jesus's life?

His Childhood

After His special birth, Jesus immediately became a target. His parents heeded a warning from an angel, and the Holy Family escaped to Egypt. Jesus began His childhood as a refugee. This detail resonates vividly as we increasingly see violence done to believers across the world.

I sometimes wonder if the gifts from the Magi from the East were useful to provide the financial means for them to flee to safety and then help them return home. Certainly Jesus spent much of His days in relative poverty. Second Corinthians 8:9 tells us, "For you know the grace of our Lord Jesus Christ, that though he was rich, yet for your sake he became poor, so that you through his poverty might become rich."

Eventually Jesus returned to His human father's hometown in Nazareth, where He worked as a carpenter like His dad, Joseph. During this time, Galilee had a housing boom. No doubt Jesus worked in the cities of the Decapolis, the ten Roman cities encircling the beautiful Sea of Galilee.

During His ministry on earth, Jesus made Capernaum His base. Today Capernaum is still called "Jesus Town" by locals on the northern banks of the small sea, thirteen miles by eight miles in dimension. Jesus's humble labor as a carpenter honors those who work hard with their hands.

His Character

We know more from the Bible about Jesus's character than His physical accomplishments during His youth. He "grew in wisdom and stature, and in favor with God and man" (Luke 2:52). He "learned obedience" (Hebrews 5:8). He traveled on foot in a caravan of extended family to Jerusalem for the festivals, where as a twelve-year-old He amazed the religious leaders with His understanding (Luke 2:41–50). He read the Scriptures in the synagogue (Luke 4:16–21).

Jesus was a practicing Jew, living under Roman law and occupation. No doubt He saw some of His friends spit where Roman soldiers had trod, but Jesus loved His enemies. He was never bitter, even toward those who wanted to harm Him.

We know even more of Jesus's character from His ministry. He was strong, self-controlled, and filled with the Spirit. He was humble yet courageous. He was caring. The line of people who wanted to talk to Him never seemed to end, yet He was wise enough to pull away from the crowds to reflect and renew His devotion to the Father and the Father's will, always His guiding relationship and principle. Jesus was obedient and suffered even to the cross, yet He remained the most gracious man of all.

There has never been a man more perfect than Jesus. He never sinned. His character was tested extremely, but He withstood temptations and trials of every kind. He worked miracles.

At His birth He was worshiped.

At His bar mitzvah He astounded the wisest men in the nation.

During His ministry, crowds flocked around Him despite His attempts to keep His great miracles quiet. On His final entry to Jerusalem the crowds went into a frenzy over Him.

He made the other heroes of the day jealous because He was so popular. But Jesus had the purest of characters, and He never flinched from His purpose.

He passed the test of suffering and success. No one has ever been able to damage His character.

His Sinlessness

One phrase summarizes Jesus's entire time on earth: *He never sinned.* This is evident to readers of the Gospels. The book of Hebrews also states clearly that in Jesus's quest for obedience, He was sinless:

> Therefore, since we have a great high priest who has ascended into heaven, Jesus the Son of God, let us hold firmly to the faith we profess. For we do not have a high priest who is unable to empathize with our weaknesses, but we have one who has been tempted in every way, just as we are—yet he did not sin. Let us then approach God's throne of grace with confidence, so that we may receive mercy and find grace to help us in our time of need. (Hebrews 4:14–16)

The One and Only was a unique person—all human and all God. He was tempted in every way as we are. (Yes, every way.) But there is one difference between Jesus and us: He never sinned. *Never*. Though He was tempted to lust, He did not succumb. Women felt safe around Him. Men who truly knew Him respected Him. He achieved what money could never buy: self-control, contentment, and godliness.

The fact that Jesus led a sinless life also means He never committed the sins of omission. Many of our sins are the things we do not do—such as the good we could have done, the words we could have spoken, or the stand we could have taken. Consider the good you could have done but didn't, the conversations you could have had but left unsaid, and the time you have wasted. Jesus did not commit any of those sins. He wasted nothing. Yet Jesus knew how to rest. He remained in perfect communion with His Father. Yes, He was stretched at times. Crowds pushed, disciples failed, and soldiers taunted and bullied. But He knew to slip away to spend time resting and being refreshed by His heavenly Father.

It is not a sin to be tempted or tried. Jesus never sinned. He went to the cross without sin and then became sin for us:

> God made him who had no sin to be sin for us, so that in him we might become the righteousness of God. (2 Corinthians 5:21)

This makes me want to follow Him all the more. What a man! What a Savior! Only God's Son could do this. We could not have a Savior who had sinned; how then would a sinner save sinners? He was an unblemished Lamb sacrificed for us. This is the glorious wonder of His life. Not only did Jesus avoid falling short of God's standard, but He also fulfilled His saving purpose.

JESUS'S WORDS

One of my favorite characters in revival history is Evan Roberts, the famed "praying preacher" of the 1904–05 Welsh Revival. I have read all I can about Evan and have even walked in his footsteps and have preached where he preached. Only one seven-second recording of his voice exists. My heart beat faster when I first heard it, and I played those few seconds over and over.

Jesus preached the greatest and perhaps most influential words ever spoken, yet we have never heard His physical voice. What would it have been like to hear air moving through His vocal cords, forming sounds into words?

No doubt people were amazed at His words. Jesus spoke "as one who had authority" (Matthew 7:29). This does not mean He was authoritarian but that He knew His subject and He delivered it with a power that was utterly convincing. He lived His message. He taught with kindness, helpfulness, and power. We all aim for a balance, but He is the only One who has ever balanced truth and grace perfectly.

Jesus spoke the greatest words ever spoken:

> Let your light shine before others, that they may see your good deeds and glorify your Father in heaven. (Matthew 5:16)

Turn . . . the other cheek. (Matthew 5:39)

Love your enemies. (Matthew 5:44)

But seek first his kingdom and his righteousness, and all these things will be given to you as well. Therefore do not worry about tomorrow, for tomorrow will worry about itself. Each day has enough trouble of its own. (Matthew 6:33–34)

Do not judge, or you too will be judged. (Matthew 7:1)

Do to others what you would have them do to you. (Matthew 7:12)

Give back to Caesar what is Caesar's, and to God what is God's. (Matthew 22:21)

It is not the healthy who need a doctor, but the sick. I have not come to call the righteous, but sinners. (Mark 2:17)

Let any one of you who is without sin be the first to throw a stone. (John 8:7)

I am the resurrection and the life. (John 11:25)

Jesus spoke the Beatitudes, the parables, the Lord's Prayer, and His powerful words from the cross. When we read our

Bibles, we must be familiar not just with the red letters that distinguish the words Jesus spoke, but also with all the words of Scripture that He believed, quoted, and fulfilled.

Jesus's words endure. His words are life.

> Everyone who hears these words of mine and puts them into practice is like a wise man who built his house on the rock. (Matthew 7:24)

JESUS'S MIRACLES

When I was school in the UK, we had religious education every week—and sometimes every day. This subject usually included Bible stories. One of my teachers encouraged us to think deeply about the stories we were learning. For example, in a discussion about Jesus walking on the water, the teacher asked us to come up with ways that this miracle could be explained away by something in the natural world. We all agreed that there was no doubt that the disciples thought a genuine, supernatural miracle had happened. So what could be the logical or rational explanation that would show their faith false?

Perhaps Jesus was walking in shallow water.

Perhaps the disciples were drunk.

Maybe Jesus was walking on a submerged, man-made jetty.

We went on and on. Each of our suggestions became more and more farfetched.

At the time, we lived by the sea. My brother was a fisherman. Clearly the disciples who were fishermen were in their element when this miracle occurred. My classmates and I realized that these fishermen knew the sea better than anyone. The more my fellow students and I tried to think of a rational explanation to discredit the miracle of Jesus walking on the water, the more irrational we became.

The explanation posed initially by the disciples was even more irrational: "When they saw him walking on the lake, they thought he was a ghost" (Mark 6:49).

In our class that day, all our rational attempts to explain away the miracle were easily disproven. At the end of the discussion we arrived at the most logical conclusion: Jesus was as real as could be, walking on the water in the middle of a lake with winds and waves roaring.

Two years after that reasoning experiment, I accepted the Word of God as true and without error. The Bible is true. Jesus is a miracle worker because He is who the Bible says He is.

Jesus worked such a variety of miracles that the apostle John wrote that all Jesus's wonders couldn't be described in all the books of the world (John 21:25). The biblical record is the tip of the iceberg when it comes to Jesus's miracles.

We can divide His miracles into several types. First, there were miracles showing His power over creation. This includes Jesus turning the water into wine (John 2) and the calming of the storm (Mark 4).

Second, Jesus's miracles showed His power over sickness. There were times when it seemed that all night and all day people came to Him and were healed. Specifically, we see Him healing the blind (John 9), healing the paralyzed

(Mark 2), healing the deaf and unable to speak (Mark 7), healing lepers (Luke 17), and even raising people from the dead (John 11).

Third, Jesus's miracles showed His power over perfect and impossible timing. In Mark 5, He healed two people in two different places. He was not constrained by geographic location.

Fourth, Jesus's miracles showed His power over the devil and his evil schemes. He set free those who were possessed by demons (Mark 5), and He was able to pass through a hostile crowd unharmed (Luke 4).

Perhaps Jesus's greatest miracle occurred when He went to the cross, died to pay the penalty for sinners, and on the third day rose again, just as He said He would!

As we study Jesus's miracles we see farther and clearer. Like a sailor sighting land through his extending telescope after a long voyage, we smile as we begin to see that the destination is in sight.

JESUS'S CLAIMS

It is a myth that Jesus was merely a good teacher. A good teacher would never claim to be God unless it were true. So if Jesus was not God—as He said He was—then He was either delusional or a nasty deceiver. He cannot be both good and delusional; nor can He be good and a liar. The only way for Jesus to be good is if, in fact, He is who He claimed to be.

What did He claim? In John's Gospel, Jesus used the phrase "I am" seven times to explain His identity. These are called the seven "I am" sayings of Jesus. These are significant because the specific phrase "I am" that Jesus used was understood by Jews in His day to refer to the most holy name of God (Exodus 3:14). Here they are:

- "I am the bread of life. Whoever comes to me will never go hungry, and whoever believes in me will never be thirsty." (John 6:35)

- "I am the light of the world. Whoever follows me will never walk in darkness, but will have the light of life." (John 8:12)

- "I am the gate; whoever enters through me will be saved. They will come in and go out, and find pasture." (John 10:9)

- "I am the good shepherd. The good shepherd lays down his life for the sheep." (John 10:11)

- "I am the resurrection and the life. The one who believes in me will live, even though they die; and whoever lives by believing in me will never die." (John 11:25–26)

- "I am the way and the truth and the life. No one comes to the Father except through me." (John 14:6)

- "I am the vine; you are the branches. If you remain in me and I in you, you will bear much fruit; apart from me you can do nothing." (John 15:5)

In each of these statements, Jesus was claiming to be God. There are several other places in Scripture that record Jesus's claims to be God (John 4:26; 8:58; 14:11). Everything Jesus did in the Gospels declared His great humility yet also His deity.

How could so many people be persuaded by Jesus? Could it be that He was who He said He was? Many claimed to be the Messiah and were obviously not. But only Jesus truly lived such a brilliant life that He fit the bill in every way.

JESUS'S PRAYER LIFE

One day Jesus went out to pray, which was His pattern. He left before the sun that He created had risen. Jesus loved to be with people, whether teaching His disciples or ministering to the ever-increasing crowd. But He also needed time alone with His Father. This was His rhythm: time with the Father, then time with the people. On this day He was alone with God very early in the morning, but He was not so far away that the disciples couldn't find Him.

The disciples told Jesus that the crowd wanted Him. He was the answer to the world's problems, so why was He alone and not with the people? Their implication was that Jesus should always be available for people. There even seems to be a hint of rebuke from the disciples.

But Jesus replied that He and the disciples needed to go somewhere else. There were other people who needed to meet Him. How did He know this? Through prayer (Mark 1:35–38).

Prayer takes us deep and sends us out into the world.

Prayer is a challenging journey. But no one did it better than Jesus, and He must be our teacher.

After observing Jesus's prayer life for a while, the disciples asked Jesus to teach them how to pray (Luke 11:1). We all need to learn this. Sometimes prayer is easy, but often it is hard. We often suffer from distraction, and we can be too busy.

Jesus gave us the model prayer as an example for all of us:

This, then, is how you should pray:
"Our Father in heaven,
hallowed be your name,
your kingdom come,
your will be done,
on earth as it is in heaven.
Give us today our daily bread.
And forgive us our debts,
as we also have forgiven our debtors.
And lead us not into temptation,
but deliver us from the evil one."
(Matthew 6:9–13)

Through His prayer life, Jesus demonstrated that He lived in perfect communion with His Father.

JESUS'S MEDIATION

Jesus clearly helped people know God. He restored people's broken relationships with God as He helped them through His teaching, His love, and His healing. But most of all, Jesus was our mediator through His death and resurrection.

The way Jesus gave His love to us was through the cross. To talk of blood may seem a strange thing. It reminds us of animal sacrifice—a practice that many religions understand and practice. But somehow this seems crude and ineffective to our consciences. Indeed, the relief of an animal sacrifice is only temporary. In the Old Testament, sin was temporarily removed by animal sacrifice. But hearts were not fully transformed.

Hebrews 9:22 explains, "The law requires that nearly everything be cleansed with blood, and without the shedding of blood there is no forgiveness."

Finally, the sin problem of the world was answered once and for all through the sacrifice of Jesus. The former sacrificial system in the Old Testament paved the way for Jesus Christ to be the ultimate, final fulfillment as a sacrifice. Just as a lamb was sacrificed in the Old Testament, so Jesus is our "Passover lamb" (1 Corinthians 5:7).

When Jesus died on the cross, He was accomplishing a unique thing. He took upon Himself the punishment that sinners deserved to bring mankind to God.

- "He was oppressed and afflicted, yet he did not open his mouth; he was led like a lamb to the slaughter, and as a sheep before its shearers is silent, so he did not open his mouth." (Isaiah 53:7)

- "In him we have redemption through his blood, the forgiveness of sins, in accordance with the riches of God's grace." (Ephesians 1:7)

- "But now he has reconciled you by Christ's physical body through death to present you holy in his sight, without blemish and free from accusation." (Colossians 1:22)

It is through the mediation of Jesus that we are forgiven. This means that Jesus is the One who brings together God and mankind in a restored relationship.

The great preacher Charles Spurgeon once said, "Through Jesus' blood there is not a spot left upon any believer, not a wrinkle nor any such thing. Oh precious blood, removing the hell-stains of abundant iniquity, and permitting me to stand accepted in the beloved, notwithstanding all the many ways which I have rebelled against my God."[1]

Sometimes in our culture the cross of Jesus Christ is turned into merely a religious symbol. The true significance of the cross, though, is vast. Scripture tells us what was truly accomplished on the cross:

For God was pleased to have all his fullness dwell in [Jesus], and through him to reconcile to himself all things, whether things on earth or things in heaven, by making peace through his blood, shed on the cross. (Colossians 1:19–20)

You see, at just the right time, when we were still powerless, Christ died for the ungodly. Very rarely will anyone die for a righteous person, though for a good person someone might possibly dare to die. But God demonstrates his own love for us in

this: While we were still sinners, Christ died for us
(Romans 5:6–8)

The life of the One and Only is available to all of us who
believe because of His sacrifice for my sins, your sins, our
sins—everybody's sins. We can have faith in Jesus. Believe
in Him and do not doubt.

Jesus was designated in heaven as the mediator between
God and humans. Scripture says, "For there is one God and
one mediator between God and mankind, the man Christ
Jesus" (1 Timothy 2:5). Jesus Christ is forever our only hope
and forever the only way to salvation and eternal life. He is
the One and Only. Jesus is God.

DID JESUS RISE
FROM THE DEAD?

In this book we are asking questions that help us understand the Grand Story. We began with the analogy of a
extending telescope, each truth fitting with the others so
that as we add each section, we can see more clearly.

So far in this book we have studied creation, the reality
of right and wrong, the reliability of the Bible, and the fact
that Jesus is God. Now we will consider the question: "Did
Jesus rise from the dead?" If we can believe these things happened—and they did—then what truth, what a foundation!

In this chapter, the focus will stay on the central figure
of the Grand Story. Jesus was never a soldier, but He suffered at the hands of Roman soldiers. He never held public
office, but He is the greatest leader of all time. He died for
our sin, but three days later, as prophesied in the Scriptures
and by Jesus Himself, He rose again.

I am grateful that when I was attending an evangelical
seminary in London, we occasionally studied the writings of

those who held a different view of Scripture. One of them was Rudolf Bultmann, the poster-child of liberal theology in the early twentieth century. Liberal theology is not a political term; it refers to disbelieving the divine authorship of the Bible.

Bultmann originally was an evangelist. This man, who would later become notorious for challenging those with a Bible-believing faith, really did want people to believe in Jesus Christ. But he could also see that many people were turning away from the old truths of the Christian faith. Universities were teaching evolution and secularism. The key word of the day was *reason*. The supernatural was not considered to be rational or believable and thus disregarded. This led to a strange circular argument: because miracles do not usually happen, they cannot happen. (But isn't that the point of a miracle? To be something that doesn't usually happen?) As Bultmann observed the changes in society, with people trusting the Bible less and less, he tried to eliminate the things in the Bible that people found hard to believe.

Many modern preachers are doing the same thing today. They eliminate that which is difficult, ignore the tough passages, and submit to the cultural trends of believing only the socially acceptable parts of the Bible. If a truth is less acceptable, then they don't mention it to their congregations. In their sermons they strive to cause no offense—even though the very means of our salvation, the cross, is an offense! Hence, many churches today refer less to the Bible. They preach less "it is written." This is a slippery slope.

Rudolf Bultmann cut away at the Bible. Because he saw

the supernatural as nonessential, he disbelieved the miracles, including the virgin birth. The result of his selective trimmings causes us to ask, who was this Jesus, then, and can He save? Predictably, Bultmann denied Jesus's bodily resurrection because it was supernatural. It was as if he were trying to remove the appendix to make things easier, but instead he took away the heart and lungs. So Bultmann claimed the resurrection of Jesus Christ did not happen.

Subsequent church leaders have talked of the "Jesus of faith" instead of the resurrected Jesus. Behind this shift in vocabulary is a shift in belief. They say, "Jesus did not actually rise from the dead, but it is okay for Christians to keep the notion of the resurrection alive." Or, "We like to think Jesus is alive, but we know He isn't." This is nothing more than wishful-thinking theology.

When it comes to the issue of the resurrection of Jesus Christ, the question is not "Is it acceptable?" or "Is it popular?" but "Is it true?" Did the resurrection really happen?

ARGUMENTS AGAINST THE RESURRECTION

Old arguments against the resurrection of Jesus Christ re-emerge every so often. Some people object that the story of Jesus's resurrection was written in the Bible merely as myth. Other arguments against the resurrection of Jesus arise from the naturalist's view: "Because resurrection doesn't happen in the natural world, it did not happen for Jesus."

But the biblical evidence says Jesus did rise from the dead. So the naturalists have to explain this historical evidence. Their theories of what they think really happened read like an Agatha Christie or Sherlock Holmes whodunit.

1. The Pathetic Disciples Theory

Some of those who oppose the resurrection assume that Jesus's disciples were easily fooled. They claim the apostles were not very bright. Forget that some of the disciples were fishermen like my brother, who is one of the most practical people I know. Many naturalists assume a subpar intelligence of the disciples that is not historic or accurate. They say things like:

"The resurrection story must have been exaggerated."

"The disciples wanted the resurrection to be true. It was wish fulfillment."

"The disciples were grief-stricken after the cross. It was their imagination."

The followers of Jesus included Luke, considered to be one of the most credible historians of his day. Many people in Jesus's close circle of disciples were not natural men of faith. This group included, deniers like Peter and doubters like Thomas. They didn't want to believe. The disciples took some persuading, but eventually they were so convinced that Jesus was the Messiah that they all were willing to follow Jesus and die for Him.

The disciples who were fishermen—like my brother, who has been known to occasionally be skeptical—were tough fellows. They could fish all night in terrible weather. They were have-to-see-it-to-believe-it types. These were hard men to fool.

Some clergymen propose that the disciples merely conjured up the "Jesus of faith," meaning that the resurrection didn't happen but the disciples liked the idea of it, so they made it up and started telling others about it. But does it make sense that these men held fast to the resurrection amid intense persecution and ended up as martyrs, giving their lives for a story that they had known to be a lie?

Worse still, some disbelievers say the resurrection of Jesus was merely an emotional episode by the grief-stricken disciples. In other words, the resurrection was nothing more than a group psychotic hallucination. Now, such a thing can happen to one person if he or she has mental or psychotic issues. But it is impossible for two or more people to have the same imagined experience. There is no such thing as a group hallucination.

Still other skeptics say that the resurrection was a ghost appearance, or perhaps a UFO. We are getting irrational now!

The problem with all of these theories is that the Bible is clear that the resurrected Jesus ate with the disciples (Luke 24:41–43). He showed them His hands and side, which had been pierced during His crucifixion (John 20:20). He appeared at least nine times to various people after they witnessed His death, to more than five hundred people at one occurrence (1 Corinthians 15:6).

2. The Swap Theory

Other people who reject the resurrection of Jesus have developed something called the swap theory. The swap theory has two possibilities: (1) Jesus of Nazareth died but then someone else pretended to be the resurrected Jesus, or (2) someone else died in Jesus's place and three days later Jesus appeared and then disappeared. In either scenario, the whole resurrection miracle was a con, and Jesus was in on it.

In the first instance, the swapped person would have had to look and act exactly like Jesus to convince friends and family of His resurrection when they were most inclined to disbelieve it. In the second instance, this swapped person would have had to look the same as Jesus and die in His place. The Gospels confirm that Jesus's own mother was at the crucifixion, so the swapped person would have had to fool Jesus's mother! The apostle John, one of Jesus's closest friends, was also there. There are multiple eyewitness accounts of Jesus's death and resurrection. If the swap theory were true, then this plot fooled everybody, including His closest friends and His own mother.

Was Jesus swapped with another person before the cross? If so, He must have hidden somewhere during the crucifixion and then reappeared, pretending to have been resurrected.

There are several problems with the swap theory. First, if the resurrection was just a body-swap, then the Christian faith is a vile hoax and all Christians should be pitied (I Corinthians 15:19).

Another problem with this theory is that the swapped Jesus ascended to heaven in front of the apostles, who were utterly convinced of all these events, His body double must have been a greater miracle-worker than the actual Jesus!

If the true Jesus went into hiding, as one form of the swap theory suggests, then He was a coward. The One who had said, "Do to others what you would have them do to you" (Matthew 7:12) tried to avoid pain, in contrast to the biblical witness that said He took punishment in the place of others (I Peter 2:24).

Would we think that Jesus told us to serve and give yet selfishly walked away and let some other poor fellow die in His place? If that were true, then everything He preached was all a lie, an utter hoax.

The truth is that no one died in Jesus's place. Instead, He died in our place.

3. The Swoon Theory

The swoon theory claims that Jesus didn't actually die. The Man on the cross may have been injured, but He suffered no life-threatening injuries. Is that possible? Let's consider the extent of Jesus's sufferings and injuries recorded in all four Gospels and referenced throughout the New Testament.

In the Garden of Gethsemane, as Jesus considered the imminence of His arrest and death, He sweat drops of blood (Luke 22:44). This could have been the same medical condition that soldiers were known to have in World War I. As a fresh charge was commanded and the troops were about to leave the trenches to go to an almost certain death, some soldiers were known to sweat blood as the capillaries in their foreheads burst due to the intensity of the moment.

So already greatly stressed, though obedient and strengthened by angels, Jesus was arrested and taken to the house of Caiaphas, the Jewish high priest. Jesus was interrogated there and stayed the night under guard, and He was probably thrown in a pit after being beaten.

Then Jesus was beaten intensely throughout the day of His trial. He was repeatedly hit in the face and whipped by rods. He endured a Jewish flogging at night and a Roman beating in the morning.

The Roman flagellum was known to take men to within an inch of their lives. Many prisoners died during their floggings. The Roman soldiers used a whip—threaded with pieces of metal and bone—that would stick on the flesh. A skilled operator would then rip the flesh from the body, resulting in severe trauma and blood loss. Some prisoners would die of shock as the body convulsed during this flogging. As we consider the horrific torture Jesus endured, and understand how weak His body was before He ever went to the cross, we begin to realize how bizarre and unrealistic the swoon theory is becoming.

Jesus then was forced to carry His wooden cross at least several hundred yards. That would have taken some time. His body was breaking down so much that Simon of Cyrene was commanded to help (Mark 15:21).

When Jesus arrived at the execution scene, He was nailed to a cross. They pierced His hands and feet. He suffered more blood loss, shock, and agony.

Then He was lifted up and hung in a public place for six hours. He had open wounds, with blood dripping. He suffered exhaustion. His body was positioned for maximum exposure to the heat. He had great difficulty breathing through the pain.

All four Gospels record that Jesus suffered greatly and then died.

Is a swoon here possible? Remember, the Roman soldiers were not done yet with the damage to His physical body and organs. The death squad monitored His body during the crucifixion. At the command of the centurion, soldiers pierced Jesus's side with a large spear. "Blood and water" flowed from His side—medical proof of His death (John 19:34). I have heard it suggested over the years that the custom of the Roman army was that if a prisoner escaped, the entire squad would be killed, in keeping with Rome's totalitarian military. They clearly were not going to get this wrong.

After Jesus's final breath, the lead Roman centurion, who had watched how He died, said, "Surely this man was the Son of God!" (Mark 15:39). This lead soldier was not only convinced that Jesus was dead, but he was overwhelmed with the godliness and even deity of Jesus from the way He died.

Proponents of the swoon theory say that at this point Jesus was taken down from the cross still alive, although the Romans and His family and friends were convinced otherwise.

This theory says the Romans were fools. They say that the "resurrection" that occurred three days later was actually just a reappearance of the same man, who had never actually died. Maybe Jesus went to the ICU for a couple of nights?

But this so-called falsely resurrected One could walk, talk, and eat easily—despite being pierced by a spear that penetrated His side and His heart, and despite all the other cuts and trauma to His body. What secret medical help could the Man on the cross have received to be in such great physical condition in only three days?

Surely it is rational to study the certainty of a victim's

death as a result of crucifixion, especially the most recorded of all crucifixions. Jesus did not die in secret but in the glare of the public. Hundreds must have seen it, if not thousands.

You see, those who make up these theories don't often apply much science, historic reason, or logic to their attempts at finding a seemingly "rational" explanation. Despite huge nails plunged through His feet, they say that Jesus could walk perfectly with no limp. They say He was physically strong, despite His blood loss and trauma. There was no bleeding from His hundreds of wounds or permanent damage to His internal organs.

Can we really consider the swap or swoon theories as credible or rational?

Bultmann and many others say there must be a reasonable explanation for the carefully told resurrection story in the Gospels. They think that, like an episode of *Scooby Doo*, something that appeared to be supernatural actually had a natural explanation behind it. All four Gospels, however, leave no room for doubt about the resurrection of Jesus Christ. Jesus's after-death appearances were neither a ghost nor a swap nor a swoon. It was a bodily resurrection.

EVIDENCE FOR THE RESURRECTION

I encourage any who doubt the resurrection to investigate closely the resurrection accounts in the Bible. Just Matthew's story is enough.

1. Jesus Claimed to Be God

Through careful study of the Scriptures, Jesus is proclaimed as the unique Son of God and is therefore divine. Jesus claimed this both overtly and by implication throughout His ministry.

The relationship between the Father and the Son is repeated often in John's Gospel but also elsewhere. For instance, in Matthew 11, Jesus made as bold a claim as possible to be God, always demonstrated humbly as an obedient Son. Tom Smail, in his classic book *The Forgotten Father*, zoomed in on verse 27 as Matthew's decisive moment, revealing the relationship between Father and Son.[1]

> All things have been committed to me by my Father. No one knows the Son except the Father, and no one knows the Father except the Son and those to whom the Son chooses to reveal him. (Matthew 11:27)

This verse is key to understanding Jesus's relationship to the Father. The three words that follow in verse 28, "Come to me," are our response to the revealed Son. He is the One and Only, and we must turn to Him:

> Come to me, all you who are weary and burdened, and I will give you rest. Take my yoke upon you and learn from me, for I am gentle and humble in heart, and you will find rest for your souls. For my yoke is easy and my burden is light. (Matthew 11:28–30)

2. Jesus Prophesied His Own Death and Resurrection

Neither Jesus's death nor His resurrection took Him by surprise. Even though those closest to Him failed to understand fully this prophecy before it played out, Jesus had told them what was coming.

> From that time on Jesus began to explain to his disciples that he must go to Jerusalem and suffer many things at the hands of the elders, the chief priests and the teachers of the law, and that he must be killed and on the third day be raised to life.
>
> Peter took him aside and began to rebuke him. "Never, Lord!" he said. "This shall never happen to you!"
>
> Jesus turned and said to Peter, "Get behind me, Satan! You are a stumbling block to me; you do not have in mind the concerns of God, but merely human concerns." (Matthew 16:21–23)

> Now Jesus was going up to Jerusalem. On the way, he took the Twelve aside and said to them, "We are going up to Jerusalem, and the Son of Man will be delivered over to the chief priests and the teachers of the law. They will condemn him to death and will hand him over to the Gentiles to be mocked and flogged and crucified. On the third day he will be raised to life!" (Matthew 20:17–19)

3. Jesus's Death Occurred in Open View of the Public

All four Gospels record that Jesus died on the cross in plain view of many eyewitnesses, some of whom were His followers and many others who opposed Him. The Acts of the

Apostles, which tells of the events directly following Jesus's resurrection, repeatedly focuses on His death. Almost every New Testament letter focuses on Jesus's death as well.

Matthew gave the following account of the moment when Jesus died, noting the presence of many witnesses to Jesus's crucifixion:

> Two rebels were crucified with him, one on his right and one on his left. Those who passed by hurled insults at him, shaking their heads and saying, "You who are going to destroy the temple and build it in three days, save yourself! Come down from the cross, if you are the Son of God!" In the same way the chief priests, the teachers of the law and the elders mocked him. "He saved others," they said, "but he can't save himself! He's the king of Israel! Let him come down now from the cross, and we will believe in him. He trusts in God. Let God rescue him now if he wants him, for he said, 'I am the Son of God.'" In the same way the rebels who were crucified with him also heaped insults on him.
>
> From noon until three in the afternoon darkness came over all the land. About three in the afternoon Jesus cried out in a loud voice, "*Eli, Eli, lema sabachthani?*" (which means "My God, my God, why have you forsaken me?").
>
> When some of those standing there heard this, they said, "He's calling Elijah."
>
> Immediately one of them ran and got a sponge.

He filled it with wine vinegar, put it on a staff, and offered it to Jesus to drink. The rest said, "Now leave him alone. Let's see if Elijah comes to save him."

And when Jesus had cried out again in a loud voice, he gave up his spirit. (Matthew 27:38–50)

4. Unusual Activities in Nature Occurred During Jesus's Death and Resurrection

If the Son of God died and rose again to life, you would expect something astounding to happen in the natural world. And in fact, it did:

At that moment the curtain of the temple was torn in two from top to bottom. The earth shook, the rocks split and the tombs broke open. The bodies of many holy people who had died were raised to life. They came out of the tombs after Jesus' resurrection and went into the holy city and appeared to many people.

When the centurion and those with him who were guarding Jesus saw the earthquake and all that had happened, they were terrified, and exclaimed, "Surely he was the Son of God!" (Matthew 27:51–54)

Dead people came alive. The curtain in the temple was torn in two. Death could not stop Him. Jesus is alive!

5. The Record Names Witnesses

The Bible names the people who were present at the cross on the day that Jesus died, including the chief priest and elders, the apostle John, His mother, Mary, and Mary Magdalene. The presence of women further adds to the authenticity test. At that time, the culture ignored the testimony of women, so if someone in that society were trying to create and perpetrate a hoax, Matthew would have left out the names of the women or perhaps replaced them in the story with men as legally credible witnesses.

In addition to the women, the Roman centurion was there, as were the Roman death squads, Nicodemus, and Joseph of Arimathea. All of these people had a stake in getting this right.

> Many women were there, watching from a distance. They had followed Jesus from Galilee to care for his needs. Among them were Mary Magdalene, Mary the mother of James and Joseph, and the mother of Zebedee's sons.
>
> As evening approached, there came a rich man from Arimathea, named Joseph, who had himself become a disciple of Jesus. (Matthew 27:55–57)

6. Pilate Released the Dead Body

Pilate released the body of Jesus, the state's enemy, because he no longer thought Him a threat.

> Going to Pilate, he [Joseph of Arimathea] asked for Jesus' body, and Pilate ordered that it be given to him. Joseph took the body, wrapped it in a clean linen cloth, and placed it in his own new tomb that he had cut out of the rock. He rolled a big stone in

front of the entrance to the tomb and went away.
Mary Magdalene and the other Mary were sitting
there opposite the tomb. (Matthew 27:58–61)

7. The Pharisees Insisted That Romans Guard Jesus's Tomb

Because they knew Jesus had prophesied His resurrection,
the Pharisees took careful precaution to prevent any deception or hoax. So they arranged for Roman soldiers to guard
the tomb where Jesus's body had been placed:

> The next day, the one after Preparation Day, the
> chief priests and the Pharisees went to Pilate. "Sir,"
> they said, "we remember that while he was still alive
> that deceiver said, 'After three days I will rise again.'
> So give the order for the tomb to be made secure un-
> til the third day. Otherwise, his disciples may come
> and steal the body and tell the people that he has
> been raised from the dead. This last deception will
> be worse than the first."
>
> "Take a guard," Pilate answered. "Go, make the
> tomb as secure as you know how." So they went and
> made the tomb secure by putting a seal on the stone
> and posting the guard. (Matthew 27:62–66)

What did the Roman guards say had happened at the
tomb? Jesus rose. The report threatened the religious
leaders so much that they paid the soldiers to lie. The
Pharisees had taken every precaution to keep a hoax from

happening. The soldiers had vigilantly guarded the tomb at risk of their lives for dereliction of duty. Yet the actions and words of Jesus's enemies confirm that their worst fear had occurred—resurrection.

> While the women were on their way, some of the guards went into the city and reported to the chief priests everything that had happened. When the chief priests had met with the elders and devised a plan, they gave the soldiers a large sum of money, telling them, "You are to say, 'His disciples came during the night and stole him away while we were asleep.' If this report gets to the governor, we will satisfy him and keep you out of trouble." So the soldiers took the money and did as they were instructed. And this story has been widely circulated among the Jews to this very day. (Matthew 28:11–15)

Some still refuse to believe no matter how strong the evidence is for resurrection. We have to wonder: When these people ask the question, "Did Jesus rise from the dead," do they really want the answer?

8. Jesus Appeared Nine Times Post-Resurrection

The Bible records that Jesus appeared nine times after the resurrection. How did the disciples, a group of fearful men, become so bold and courageous in such a short space of time? Before the Easter events they seemed to cower in fear. Most of us understand the power of fear to cripple us. But a short time after Jesus's crucifixion, they were on the streets proclaiming His resurrection.

The gift of the Holy Spirit that they received on the Day of Pentecost, fifty days after the Passover when Jesus sacrificed Himself, was a confirmation that Jesus is alive and He lives in us! The disciples knew this first because they saw Him alive, just as He had promised, and they were overjoyed!

9. The Apostles Gained Unshakeable Courage and Persistence

All of the apostles (except Judas Iscariot) died for the faith. Legend holds that Matthew was killed by a sword in Ethiopia, Luke was hanged in Greece, Peter was crucified upside down in Rome, James was thrown down from the temple, and Thomas was speared in India.

Ever since, thousands have willingly died for the risen and ascended One. We are hearing more and more about Christians who are being martyred for their faith in Jesus. These followers of Christ are imprisoned, attacked, mocked, and beaten. But nothing can stop them from sharing Jesus. I pray for the same courage for you and me.

10. Paul's Conversion Shows Skeptics Can Believe

The apostle Paul, formerly Saul of Tarsus, met Jesus while traveling on the Damascus Road (Acts 9). The conversion of Christianity's greatest enemy is one of the great proofs of the resurrection.

Saul of Tarsus hated Christians. Though a highly educated man, he had a bias deep in his soul. Skeptics must beware of missing the obvious. Saul was proud of his Jewish heritage. He received the highest form of training available. He was taught in the greatest schools by the greatest teachers of the day. It seems that he was a top student and was advancing rapidly in the world of Judaism.

But this deeply religious man was a bigot. He was part of an establishment that resisted what God was doing in Jesus despite His life being so clearly prophesied in Jewish Scripture.

So Saul tried to destroy the church. He gave approval for the execution of a popular Christian, and then he went house to house rounding up new believers and carting them off to prison. He was a man on a mission. The wrong mission.

Then he met Jesus! That must have been quite a shock. On the Damascus Road, while Saul was chasing Christians, Jesus appeared in blinding light to Saul and asked, "'Saul, Saul, why do you persecute me?' 'Who are you, Lord?' Saul asked. 'I am Jesus, whom you are persecuting,' he replied. 'Now get up and go into the city, and you will be told what you must do'" (Acts 9:4–6).

Later in the New Testament, Saul— now called the apostle Paul—told how this moment changed his life (1 Timothy 1:13–16). Of course, all our lives have been changed by Paul's life as he wrote or appears in approximately half the New Testament books.

Paul's conversion shows that even the toughest skeptic

can believe. None of us should rule out our own conversion. And millions more like Paul have been converted.

Jesus Christ still resurrects once spiritually dead souls, including mine. He is still working in people's lives today. There have been millions of remarkable conversions, including my own. He saved me and made me alive. I know Him. And I know He lives.

IS THERE LIFE
AFTER DEATH?

If anyone asked how a person died, my grandfather always replied that they had stopped breathing! One day my dear grandpa also stopped breathing, as you will and I will someday. The question of this chapter is the one everybody should ask: Is there life after death?

After death, what will happen to me? And to you? This is an important question. Do you see how a right understanding that our world has a Maker, a morality (right and wrong), a true Word from God, and a Savior who was both God and man and who rose from the dead, affects how we answer this question? If we have a Maker, then He created not only this life but the next. If we have a morality, then we must meet this standard in order to enter the next life. If we have a true Word from God, then it would surely tell us how to meet that standard. If we have a Savior who is both God and man, then He can reveal to us God's standard and also fulfill perfectly the moral standard that we fall so short of meeting. And if that Savior rose from the dead, He has proven that death has no hold over us and that He is able to open to us the doors of eternity.

Our destination after we die will define the rest of our days. Only one viewpoint can be correct. So how do we know what happens after we die? Who decides?

Some believe that heaven will be like what is described by the ghost stories, superstitions, or the tribal elders of the day. There used to be a time when popular movies portrayed heaven as a place in the clouds with lots of harps. I am glad those images have largely been left behind. That view of heaven was unbiblical and seemed so dull. People would think that death must be avoided at all costs if that kind of heaven is the best it gets!

The naturalists want us to believe that nothing exists after death—that we simply cease to exist. But most people generally avoid discussions about death, though to ignore death is surely to ignore an unavoidable fact of life. Like it or not, death is a reality.

My friend and fellow pastor Ike Reighard says it like this: "Life is tissue-paper thin." We must be ready for the moment of our death, though many block out the subject. People prefer to talk about almost anything other than death and life after death.

LIFE AFTER DEATH

We can learn about the reality of life after death from the words of Jesus Himself. I trust Him to tell us the truth about life after death. After all, He came from heaven to earth, went back again, and still speaks to us. Surely Jesus is the most credible source of all regarding life and death.

Jesus taught very clearly that there are two eternal destinations after death. In His story of the rich man and Lazarus, He described the comfort of heaven and warned us of the dangers of a place called Hades. Jesus pointed out that even if someone did come back from the dead to warn them of the realities of hell, many people still wouldn't listen to him.

That is one of the challenges I am giving you in this book. Are you willing to change your worldview, to repent of your sins, and to live for Christ now and forever? If so, the hope of heaven means that you and I can suffer and struggle and not be overly discouraged.

Read Jesus's words describing the reality of life after death:

There was a rich man who was dressed in purple and fine linen and lived in luxury every day. At his gate was laid a beggar named Lazarus, covered with sores and longing to eat what fell from the rich man's table. Even the dogs came and licked his sores.

The time came when the beggar died and the angels carried him to Abraham's side. The rich man also died and was buried. In Hades, where he was in torment, he looked up and saw Abraham far away, with Lazarus by his side. So he called to him, "Father Abraham, have pity on me and send Lazarus to dip the tip of his finger in water and cool my tongue, because I am in agony in this fire." (Luke 16:19–24)

We can learn much from this story. There is a heaven and a hell—and nothing in between. There is no neutral place. No purgatory. No annihilation. No soul-jail. No "nothing." Heaven is for righteous people who have been redeemed, as demonstrated in this passage. Hell is for unrighteousness people, who in an unredeemed state have no sense of compassion or justice for their fellow man.

There are only two eternal destinations, and you cannot switch your destination after you die. Wealth can buy power in life, but it has no power after death. The mafia or the media have power today but none tomorrow. Yet the believer who suffers for the Lord on the earth will have glory in heaven.

In this story, Jesus alluded to the joy of heaven, though He didn't spell out the details. In verse 22, when the poor man died, Jesus said that "the angels carried him to Abraham's side." Jesus used imagery that was familiar to His Jewish hearers. To the Jews of Jesus's day, heaven was to be at Abraham's side. Abraham symbolized the ancient covenant with God. He was the father of the nation of Israel.

So the poor man in Jesus's story exists after death. He is carried into heaven. He is safe. He is well. His suffering is over, and a new existence begins. He is now happy in heaven. (There will be no complaints or refunds needed from heaven.)

But the rich man in Jesus's story objects. Notice that he does not complain about the justice of where he is. God makes no mistakes. The rich man understands that he is getting what he deserves. None of us will ever be able to protest our eternal destination. God is the just Judge.

The rich man does, however, ask for someone to warn his relatives about the fires of hell. So the rich man, now in hell, speaks nobly. Though this is not possible for those in such a state, the parable has this scenario as part of the story.

> He answered, "Then I beg you, father, send Lazarus to my family, for I have five brothers. Let him warn them, so that they will not also come to this place of torment."
>
> Abraham replied, "They have Moses and the Prophets; let them listen to them."
>
> "No, father Abraham," he said, "but if someone from the dead goes to them, they will repent."
>
> He said to him, "If they do not listen to Moses and the Prophets, they will not be convinced even if someone rises from the dead." (Luke 16:27–31)

Jesus told us that after we die, we cannot appeal to Abraham or anyone else to tell our loved ones about the reality of the afterlife. The laws of the universe are set. Evangelism doesn't take place from hell but while we are still alive on earth. We have enough evidence available for everyone to hear about salvation and be saved. (This book attempts to do that very thing.)

There is only one back-from-death witness. Jesus's is the only back-from-the-dead story that we must factor in. In fact, it is His resurrection that makes our resurrection possible.

There is nothing I am more sure of than these facts: Jesus died, rose again, appeared, ascended, is at the right hand of the Father, gives us the Holy Spirit, and shall return. No doubt!

We can be sure today that heaven is for real because of Jesus and His Word given to us.

THE COMFORT OF HEAVEN

Is there any more comforting and encouraging subject to the believer than heaven? Heaven stops us from believing that life is all about us and what we can do. Heaven is our victory, justice, and vindication. It is God putting things right. It is the defeat of the devil and the end of sin and suffering. Heaven has no death, disease, or disaster. There will be no more sickness, sorrow, or suffering. What a great comfort that the pain that we experience today will be gone. So hang in there! Your faith will be rewarded. I love this verse: "For our light and momentary troubles are achieving for us an eternal glory that far outweighs them all" (2 Corinthians 4:17).

Yes, if you are a believer living for the Lord, then heaven is where you will be reunited with the Lord, your Maker and Savior. Oh, we will worship Jesus and sing, "Hallelujah! For our Lord God Almighty reigns" (Revelation 19:6), which means it will be far better than even the best moments on earth.

However, if you are a materialist and live merely for the things of this world, if your focus is on satisfying your selfish desires—if your life is all about you—then talk of heaven seems not only stupid but offensive. Heaven is only for dead people, right? Why would you waste time talking about heaven when your life is focused on the here and now? If you have no biblical understanding of heaven, then it is a real downer even to think about it.

VIEWS ABOUT LIFE AFTER DEATH

We have observed Jesus's teaching about life after death through His story about the rich man and Lazarus. How does Jesus's view of the afterlife compare to other views about life after death?

1. Nothingness After Death

Louise and I attended a secular funeral in the UK several years ago. We found the experience utterly miserable. The service took place in a crematorium, a common venue in England. All the other funerals I have attended have had at least some kind of respect for the Christian tradition of the nation. Most funeral services include a sense that there must be something more—perhaps including a mention of Psalm 23 or a familiar hymn.

However, on this occasion, the deceased person had requested that there be no religious references whatsoever during his funeral. Perhaps he was trying to avoid being a hypocrite because he really had no belief in God, or maybe he was angry toward God or believers.

So the service began. It was led by an avowed atheist who proclaimed at the outset that we live on only in the memories of our loved ones. He was neither convincing nor winsome. Frankly, this funeral speaker was a depressing figure.

I cannot remember whether music played or not. There

was a reading that was more like a sentimental rambling. The overall theme of the funeral was, "No hope." There was much weeping but no comfort. The end.

If you reject Christ, then at least a funeral like this one is honest. But memorializing a person who has rejected God during his life by denying God further at the funeral adds no commendation to the one who has departed. To me, it appeared that the children of the deceased found no comfort in the funeral service. My wife and I left disturbed. While the deceased man may have been endeavoring to be honest, his funeral was hopeless and dismal.

If that is where secular humanism leads us—to eternal separation from one another, to the claim that death is the depressing end—then what a miserable life! For those who believe that all life is random from the beginning, then it makes sense to believe that life is also random nothingness in the end. Many people believe that when you are dead, you are dead—and nothing more. End of story.

Yet most of humanity instinctively knows there must be something more than nothingness after we die. It is part of our design to long for more.

2. Reincarnation

A majority of the second largest nation in the world, India, believes in reincarnation. Reincarnation is the concept that after one dies, the soul or spirit begins a new life in a new body, cycle after cycle. The type of rebirth reflects how you lived in the previous life. So, for example, if you are grumpy in this life, then you could come back as a snapping turtle or an armadillo. (If an armadillo, Americans know that you won't last long on our roads!)

Many people believe in reincarnation, though I doubt if they have really thought it through. If reincarnation were true, who decides who goes where? How does this happen, and who makes it happen? What evidence is there?

Reincarnation requires a judgment on the morality of a life in order to determine in what body a person will come back in the next life. How does justice work without a just judge? If people were reincarnated after death, then there would have to be a just God deciding who comes back in what form. In fact, we have seen there is a just God, and His Word says that reincarnation doesn't happen.

If we believe that the Bible is reliable and God's Word, then the answer concerning reincarnation is plain in Hebrews 9:27: "People are destined to die once, and after that to face judgment." The logic behind the idea of reincarnation falls apart when scrutinized.

3. Ghosts

Where I come from in the UK there are lots of ghost stories, though I have never heard anything close to a convincing one. Many of these ghost stories have developed around castles. Once, on a school trip to Totnes Castle, a girl started claiming she could see a ghost. It turned out to be merely a light shining through the window!

The prevailing theory seems to be that when people die suddenly, their souls never quite settle and therefore reappear in limbo. The blockbuster movie Ghost depicts a heaven and hell, but the film conveys that being a ghost is like being in a holding tank between this life and the next for the souls of those who experienced a tragic or sudden death. Yet who decides what is tragic? Who decides what is sudden?

As believers in the Word of God, we have no doubt that whether our body dies slowly or suddenly, God is not caught by surprise. We will be resurrected even if we were beheaded, crucified, or burned like the some of the first apostles. Even if we are buried in a mass grave, cremated, or lost at sea, God will never lose a soul. Every human body perishes, but the soul is eternal.

Remember when Jesus walked on the water? The disciples thought He was a ghost (Matthew 14:26). But Jesus told them they were wrong.

What are ghosts, then? Well, if when we die we go to heaven or hell, then ghosts cannot be human souls. They are not zombies either. Though the popular television series *The Walking Dead* was filmed only a few miles from where I live, it was just pretend. Ghosts could be merely unexplained natural misunderstandings or imagination. Before I was converted, my grandmother played a Halloween trick on my sister Sophie and me by running past a window wearing a white sheet and pretending to be a ghost. My sister went white as that sheet. (Sorry, Sophie!)

Does the Bible tell us anything about ghosts? Did Jesus say, "By the way, ghosts are real"? Not at all. But the volume of claims of ghost sightings means that we cannot rule out every claim naturalistically. I believe that what people perceive as ghosts could sometimes be demonic imitations. Demons do exist. Jesus cast out demons. So did the early church.

So how do we know what happens at the point of death? Don't listen to the movie industry or to popular opinion. Not even to a sweet testimony. I counsel you not to fill your mind with junk. Fill your mind only with the truth of the Word of God. Ghosts are a distraction from eternal reality. So are vampires and zombies.

We need to believe what the Bible states clearly. The most famous Bible verse of all, John 3:16, offers eternal life—with no waiting room.

4. Near-Death Experiences

There have been quite a few stories of near-death experiences. Some of these storytellers claim to have gone to hell and some to heaven. This view also has a shaky foundation.

Christians believe that before we go to heaven, we have to die. So it is strange that there are stories in which a person supposedly temporarily dies, recovers, and then comes back with a tale to tell of what they experienced in the afterlife. We have agreed, as we extend our imaginary telescope, that the Bible is reliable. No one is better than Jesus to teach us about eternity. So we need not appeal to these near-death experiences for our understanding.

Instead, we can look and see that four writers in the Bible saw a vision of heaven: Isaiah, Ezekiel, Paul, and John. None of them died or nearly died before their vision. What they wrote about their visions is quite telling in comparison to the many books about near-death heaven "visits" today:

they focused almost completely on the glory of God rather than the fanciful details of the place.[1]

The Bible also lists several people who were brought back from the dead during Jesus's lifetime: Lazarus (John 11), the widow's son from Nain (Luke 7:11–17), and Jairus's daughter (Luke 8:50–56), to name a few. What details did they share about their experience? Absolutely none.

Don't place your hope on the words of individual people. Find your hope and understanding in what the Bible says about heaven.

5. Other Religions

Other religions express many other views about where we go when we die. This is another study in itself. Many people today claim that all religions are the same. But the fact is that most religions are significantly different. Some religions have one God, some have none, and some have many gods. That is a massive difference. The fact that different religions pray or value love does not reduce the significance of the differences. The task of this book is to focus on the seven great questions, including the uniqueness of the Bible and the fact of Jesus's resurrection. Since we have seen that Jesus's prophecy of His own resurrection came true, we know that He is the best source to tell us what happens after death.

WHAT DOES THE BIBLE SAY ABOUT LIFE AFTER DEATH?

God created us to walk with Him (Genesis 3:8). But in the garden of Eden, paradise was lost. Sin came in, and humanity was banished from God's garden. Sin brought death. We all deserve God's judgment—no exceptions.

So Jesus came by the mercy of God to bring eternal life to us through His shed blood. We must receive salvation by trusting Him and following Him.

The promise of John 3:16 is eternal life. "For God so loved the world that he gave his one and only Son, that whoever believes in him shall not perish but have eternal life." This eternal life as described in John 3:16 can be thought of in four ways.

Heaven Is a Place

The Bible teaches that heaven is an eternally safe yet thrilling place. Jesus said in John 14:

> Do not let your hearts be troubled. You believe in God; believe also in me. My Father's house has many rooms; if that were not so, would I have told you that I am going there to prepare a place for you? And if I go and prepare a place for you, I will come back and take you to be with me that you also may be where I am. (vv. 1–3)

Eternal life is when we are given a place by Abraham's side (Luke 16:22) and live in the presence of Jesus Christ. It is another existence beyond time and this world. It requires death to experience it.

Revelation 21:2 explains that heaven is a city: the "new Jerusalem." The new Jerusalem is a restored Eden, an international garden. And at the center of the city is God.

> Then the angel showed me the river of the water of life, as clear as crystal, flowing from the throne of God and of the Lamb down the middle of the great street of the city. On each side of the river stood the tree of life, bearing twelve crops of fruit, yielding its fruit every month. And the leaves of the tree are for the healing of the nations. . . . There will be no more night. They will not need the light of a lamp or the light of the sun, for the Lord God will give them light. And they will reign for ever and ever. (Revelation 22:1–2, 5)

The Bible is clear that heaven is a place.

Heaven Is an Experience

The Bible reveals that heaven is also an experience. It is a new and eternal life that overwhelms the worshiper.

> In the year that King Uzziah died, I saw the Lord, high and exalted, seated on a throne; and the train of his robe filled the temple. Above him were seraphim, each with six wings: With two wings they covered their faces, with two they covered their feet, and with two they were flying. And they were calling to one another:
>   "Holy, holy, holy is the Lord Almighty;
>   the whole earth is full of his glory."
>   At the sound of their voices the doorposts and thresholds shook and the temple was filled with smoke. (Isaiah 6:1–4)

The experience of being in heaven is also described as a wedding feast. The Bible begins and ends with a wedding. The first wedding is between Adam and Eve. The last wedding is the marriage of Christ and the church:

> Hallelujah!
>> For our Lord God Almighty reigns.
> Let us rejoice and be glad
>> and give him glory!
> For the wedding of the Lamb has come,
>> and his bride has made herself ready.
> Fine linen, bright and clean,
>> was given her to wear. (Revelation 19:6–8)

There will be much celebration and joy in heaven. The believer shall see the glory of God. Christ is exalted. Angels worship.

In heaven, those who believe in Jesus will have an eternal experience of transformation:

> But our citizenship is in heaven. And we eagerly await a Savior from there, the Lord Jesus Christ, who, by the power that enables him to bring everything under his control, will transform our lowly bodies so that they will be like his glorious body. (Philippians 3:20–21)

> He will wipe every tear from their eyes. There will be no more death or mourning or crying or pain, for the old order of things has passed away. (Revelation 21:4)

We never need to ask whether we still do certain positive things in heaven. All the ills will cease. And everything good will find its perfect fulfillment.

Sometimes we yearn to know a little more about heaven than has been revealed to us in the Bible. As a pastor I have been asked many times what heaven is like and what our lives will be like there. Often I reply that we just don't know. The Bible reveals to us very few details about heaven except that we can trust the One who rose from the dead.

If we trust God for our eternity, then thoughts of heaven encourage us. But there is a danger in an overactive imagination. Our thoughts are not yet perfected. We can therefore try to create the heaven of our own making rather than the heaven that truly exists.

So how should we imagine heaven? Wayne Triplett wrote, based on Revelation 21:1-5, "For the Christian, death is not the end of adventure but a doorway from a world where dreams and adventures shrink, to a world where dreams and adventures forever expand."[2] We must leave the details about heaven to God. Let it be enough for us that heaven is all about Jesus, the One who has always loved us.

Heaven Is Being with Jesus

Heaven is also about a Person. Heaven is being with Jesus.

Even in His most harrowing moments on the cross, words about heaven came from Jesus's parched lips—even to a thief: "Truly I tell you, today you will be with me in paradise" (Luke 23:43).

What do we need to know about heaven? Jesus is there. In heaven, we will see God face-to-face.

See that you do not despise one of these little ones. For I tell you that their angels in heaven always see the face of my Father in heaven. (Matthew 18:10)

For now we see only a reflection as in a mirror; then we shall see face to face. Now I know in part; then I shall know fully, even as I am fully known. (1 Corinthians 13:12)

Heaven Is Filled with People

Heaven will be full of every believer in history. Not only will Abraham be there along with the thief on the cross, but also the multitudes of believers throughout history will be together in heaven:

After this I heard what sounded like the roar of a great multitude in heaven shouting:
"Hallelujah!
Salvation and glory and power belong to our God." (Revelation 19:1)

All New Testament believers will be there. All Old Testament believers will also be there. All the Christians who have gone before us. Our family members who believe. Believers from all nations. All who believe.

For many, heaven will be a great reunion; for others, it will be a million introductions. We will be able to develop each relationship to its full potential.

Look on the horizon at the world we have not yet seen, a land of joy and plenty, with no more tears. A place where centuries and millennia will fly by and never end. In this distant but actual place we will have the greatest pleasure, which is to know God and have unbroken fellowship with Him. Pull out that telescope and have a good look. The time is getting closer. Your ship is coming in, a welcome is being prepared, and the celebration will never cease!

THE BASICS OF LIFE AFTER DEATH

Based on Jesus's story in Luke 16, how should we summarize life after death? Death has a finality. That is why we experience grief. There is a separation from how things were. And death brings a person to one of two destinations: either heaven by Abraham's side—or hell in agony.

In the Gospel of Luke, Jesus said plainly,

> In Hades, where [the rich man] was in torment, he looked up and saw Abraham far away, with Lazarus by his side. So he called to him, "Father Abraham, have pity on me and send Lazarus to dip the tip of his finger in water and cool my tongue, because I am in agony in this fire." (16:23–24)

In his Gospel, Matthew also described some of Jesus's words about hell:

> And if your eye causes you to stumble, gouge it out and throw it away. It is better for you to enter life with one eye than to have two eyes and be thrown into the fire of hell. (18:9)

Jesus spoke very directly of the dangers of hell. He should know, for He was there when Satan was cast out of heaven and has warned us against Satan ever since! Christians believe in the reality of a dangerous devil who is a daily reality in the world, nonetheless one who is defeated and shall be finally vanquished. Hell holds no fear for the believer.

Hell must be very real if the Son of God suffered an agonizing death to spare us such a fate and to give us eternity with God.

As we talk of heaven and hell, we need to feel a measure of urgency. If heaven is true, then it must affect everything we do. I have heard people say, "I want to go to hell to see my unbelieving loved ones. I would rather go to hell so I can be with them." I have heard those kinds of statements in Wales and England quite a bit. But let me suggest that there are no relationships in hell. You are guaranteed not to be reunited with anyone in hell, for there is no unity in hell. There is no relationship or fun. No God. No goodness. No wild parties, as some brag that they will create in hell. Hell has no creativity, even though people jest, "I'll have more fun in hell than heaven." No you won't. Hell is eternal suffering. That's why many still consider *hell* a bad word. We have to beware of mocking what is serious.

What if our loved ones had been converted without us knowing, and we went to hell intending to meet them—only to find out they had actually been saved and were in heaven? Get saved yourself. If you want to be reunited with anyone, you need the Lord. Jesus is the key.

A WORD ABOUT COMMUNICATING
WITH THE DEAD

Séances are forbidden in the Bible. It's best not even to joke about them either. The Bible forbids all forms of witchcraft. All witches claim to be good witches, of course. But the truth is that all witchcraft is evil.

In Jesus's parable of the rich man and Lazarus in Luke 16, the brothers of the rich man didn't need a séance or to communicate with the dead; they needed to believe the truth. Jesus told this parable to trust the words of the One who died and rose again. That would be Jesus!

The pinnacle of the parable is a sober reminder from Jesus.

> "No, father Abraham," [the rich man] said, "but if someone from the dead goes to them, they will repent."
>
> He said to him, "If they do not listen to Moses and the Prophets, they will not be convinced even if someone rises from the dead." (vv. 30–31)

Jesus Christ did rise from the dead, yet many people will believe anything but Jesus.

Is God being a spoilsport? No. God is protecting us from demonic influence. This parable spoken graciously by Jesus is clear: Don't go to Satan for advice. Instead, ask the One who is the resurrection and the life.

Both the Old Testament and New Testament warn against the deception of sorcery or trying to communicate with the dead:

Let no one be found among you who sacrifices their son or daughter in the fire, who practices divination or sorcery, interprets omens, engages in witchcraft, or casts spells, or who is a medium or spiritist or who consults the dead. (Deuteronomy 18:10–11)

The biblical command is to stay away from dodgy stuff, because the end for each of us is already decided:

For God did not send his Son into the world to condemn the world, but to save the world through him. Whoever believes in him is not condemned, but whoever does not believe stands condemned already because they have not believed in the name of God's one and only Son. (John 3:17–18)

Very truly I tell you, whoever hears my word and believes him who sent me has eternal life and will not be judged but has crossed over from death to life. Very truly I tell you, a time is coming and has now come when the dead will hear the voice of the Son of God and those who hear will live. For as the Father has life in himself, so he has granted the Son also to have life in himself. And he has given him authority to judge because he is the Son of Man.

Do not be amazed at this, for a time is coming when all who are in their graves will hear his voice and come out—those who have done what is good will rise to live, and those who have done what is evil will rise to be condemned. (John 5:24–29)

ON BEING READY

In one sense our eternity will be a surprise. But the Word helps us know the big picture. The Bible leaves some questions unanswered, but it clearly states what will happen to us after we die, without a doubt.

> Brothers and sisters, we do not want you to be uninformed about those who sleep in death, so that you do not grieve like the rest of mankind, who have no hope. For we believe that Jesus died and rose again, and so we believe that God will bring with Jesus those who have fallen asleep in him. According to the Lord's word, we tell you that we who are still alive, who are left until the coming of the Lord, will certainly not precede those who have fallen asleep. For the Lord himself will come down from heaven, with a loud command, with the voice of the archangel and with the trumpet call of God, and the dead in Christ will rise first. After that, we who are still alive and are left will be caught up together with them in the clouds to meet the Lord in the air. And so we will be with the Lord forever. Therefore encourage one another with these words. (1 Thessalonians 4:13–18)

When someone we love dies, we still weep. But if we know that our deceased loved one was a Christian, we always have hope. We will see them again in heaven. The hardest griefs I have faced have included the uncertainty of someone's spiritual condition.

This is very much a book of facts to convince your intellect, but I also appeal for your heart to be moved in response to these truths. Be touched by the fact that the human heart desires a true home.

> You guide me with your counsel,
>> and afterward you will take me into glory.
> Whom have I in heaven but you?
>> And earth has nothing I desire besides you.
> (Psalm 73:24–25)

Don't dream of a heaven without Jesus. Just focus on Jesus. Some say, "I want heaven to be a golf course with no bunkers and perfect greens." No, those things are not important. The focus of heaven is on Jesus.

As my friend says, life is tissue paper-thin. So pray for those who are lost. Pray for the salvation of friends, relatives, and neighbors today . . . and be ready yourself.

IS JESUS COMING BACK?

In this book, we have been studying the seven truths that fit together like a telescope that extends to reveal God. In this chapter we will examine the final extension of our telescope. We have come to the final question, perhaps the one that helps most to make ultimate sense of the world and the mystery of existence.

The first time I ever led a Bible study I taught from Mark's Gospel, chapter 13. I was fifteen years old. I was in a youth group meeting in Teignmouth in the southwest of England. There were about thirty of us, and many of us had come to the Lord recently. I had been a Christian for eight months. I am thankful that my youth group leader always gave us an opportunity to serve.

I was blessed not to have picked up weird notions about the last days. Not until I was converted did I even know that Jesus was coming back. I had never heard of His return, despite having daily Scripture classes in my school. But since my conversion I had heard a few sermons on the subject, so I thought I was ready to teach a Bible study about it.

Now, what is the foundational teaching on the Second Coming? We believe that all of Scripture, including the Old Testament and prophetic passages, is God's Word. But surely the best place to begin learning about the second coming of Christ is the teaching of the One who will return, the teaching from Jesus Himself in Mark 13.

I gave neither an intricate nor long Bible study to my youth group. It certainly was not clever. I had no commentaries. And I didn't have the Internet for online research. (Back then, "online" was where my mum hung the washing.)

No one taught me how to prepare a Bible study. So I read Mark 13 and prayed. I read Mark 13 again and prayed again. I didn't bring any notes because I didn't know that was an option. The Bible study hour arrived. I prayed at the beginning of the group meeting. Then we went through Mark 13, and we prayed with a sense of urgency.

I didn't add to the text. I just explained the bits I could and then said we needed to be ready. This meant we must tell our friends about Jesus—this was one thing we could do. The gospel must first be preached. I think that pretty much sums it up.

NOT "IF" BUT "WHEN"

Let's remember where we have journeyed so far in this book. These are the essential facts of the Grand Story we need to understand and carry with us each day:

1. God created the world.
2. There is a right and wrong.
3. The Bible is reliable.
4. Jesus is God.
5. Jesus did rise from the dead.
6. There is life after death.

We now ask the seventh question: "Is Jesus really coming back?"

He is. Jesus prophesied His second coming many times, and others prophesied that He would return as well. Even as Jesus ascended into heaven, two angels appeared to the many gathered there watching to reassure them that Jesus would return.

> They were looking intently up into the sky as he was going, when suddenly two men dressed in white stood beside them. "Men of Galilee," they said, "why do you stand here looking into the sky? This same Jesus, who has been taken from you into heaven, will come back in the same way you have seen him go into heaven." (Acts 1:10–11)

The apostle John, who at the Last Supper had laid his head on Jesus's chest and heard His beating heart, also declared Jesus's promised return:

> "Look, he is coming with the clouds,"
> and "every eye will see him,

even those who pierced him"; . . .
　　So shall it be! (Revelation 1:7)

The question isn't *if* Jesus will return but *when*.

THE WORDS OF JESUS

If we wanted to find out what happens at the end of the age and when it happens, where would we begin? We could ask, "Have you read a book by this author or seen that prophecy DVD?" Many Bible scholars have the end times all mapped out with charts and diagrams. Some are bolder and actually teach when Jesus's return could or could not happen. They seem to be able to turn every current event into a fulfillment of a Bible prophecy.

Now, we are to have a sense of urgency about Christ's return. As I am writing this chapter, rockets are flying from Gaza to Israel. A horrific wave of persecution against Christians is occurring in nations dominated by radical Islam. Rogue states are acquiring ever-increasing weaponry, and Russia is flexing its muscles again. The love of many for the Lord is growing cold as we experience deception and an increase in wickedness (Matthew 24:12). So how do we interpret what is going on around us?

Why not begin with the words of Jesus?

The foundational lessons of the Second Coming come from the second person of the Trinity, the Lord Jesus Christ. He is the Creator, Sustainer, and Judge of the earth. He is the only true expert when it comes to Christ's return to earth.

There is one agreed limitation to Jesus's knowledge,

which may seem unusual. Jesus, though He is all-knowing and though He is the One returning, said that there is one thing that He doesn't know! The disciples asked Him, "Tell us, when will these things happen? And what will be the sign that they are all about to be fulfilled?" (Mark 13:4). Jesus answered, "But about that day or hour no one knows, not even the angels in heaven, nor the Son, but only the Father" (v. 32).

HOW SHOULD WE PREPARE?

We often want to know when and what the signs of the last days will be. Yet Jesus spent most of His ministry addressing how we should live in the meantime. As to the question of when He will return, Jesus did not give us a specific date but submitted Himself to the Father's will.

This means that we don't need to know as much as we are tempted to know. It seems that when we lose the sense of urgency and become reliant on a tidy formula, we are claiming to know more than the One who is coming back. That is the same sin Adam and Eve fell for in the garden of Eden—wanting to know as much as (or more than) God.

Have you noticed that those who don't necessarily need to know every detail always want to be in the know? To them, information is power. Some people love to delve into the details. They want to know everything about everything.

Some people equally want to know every detail about the end times. They have to know, perhaps, because they do not trust. The subject of the end times calls for us to be trusting, humble, and zealous to do God's will. At the same time we must leave room for the mystery and sovereignty of God in all things, including the Last Days. Trusting God means going forward without knowing everything.

Perhaps some want to know the details so they can relax, assuring themselves that the end is not actually imminent so they can keep sinning or living halfheartedly in their faith. They can carry on studying but not obeying. If the end is not near, then they don't have to be ready today, do they?

Yet when it comes to the end times, ignorance is not bliss. Failing to look into these matters changes neither the day nor the hour of Jesus's return—nor our responsibility to be ready.

Revelation 5 says that Jesus is the One for whom the world eagerly awaits to reveal the mystery of the end. Yet in the Bible, Jesus told us that as to the actual time of the end, the Father alone knows the date. Jesus is the conquering King, yet He is happy to humble Himself once again on this matter. So should we. Trusting God means going forward without knowing everything.

So if someone ever assigns a time and date to the Second Coming or says Jesus's return has to happen by then, or this specific thing has to happen, or He cannot come because of this, please ask yourself, "Does this person know more than Jesus?"

The apostle Paul followed his Savior's lead in the first epistle to the Thessalonians:

> Now, brothers and sisters, about times and dates we do not need to write to you, for you know very well that the day of the Lord will come like a thief

in the night. While people are saying, "Peace and safety," destruction will come on them suddenly, as labor pains on a pregnant woman, and they will not escape. (5:1–3)

Think about it: the experts will get it wrong about when Jesus is going to return because only the Father knows the day and hour of Christ's return. That's why we need to begin with the Word and not a system. This is a good point for all scriptural interpretation. Don't allow a system or formula to trump the Word itself.

Jesus is God, but in the role He has within the Godhead, He submits to His Father, who alone will open the envelope to reveal the mystery of the second coming of Christ at the very moment of its happening.

When Jesus returns, it will be like "a thief in the night" (1 Thessalonians 5:2). The signs will be there, but it will still be unexpected. The signs of the end times are not like reading tea leaves but more like seeing a warning light. The Father gives the final signal that no one else can predict— not even Jesus.

THE SECOND COMING

Mark 13, with its parallel passage Matthew 24, is the foundational teaching on the Second Coming. Jesus taught on two events—the destruction of Jerusalem and the end of the age.

1. The Destruction of Jerusalem

Jesus predicted that the city of Jerusalem would be destroyed and the temple torn down:

> "Do you see all these great buildings?" replied Jesus. "Not one stone here will be left on another; every one will be thrown down." (Mark 13:2)

We can visit Jerusalem today and see some huge stones of the temple complex lying in ruins. The destruction of the temple happened. This prophecy was fulfilled in AD 70 when the Romans ruined the city of peace.

Jesus spoke this warning to His generation, which would see great upheaval. The destruction of the temple is still a focal point for Jews today as they pray and welcome others to pray at the Western Wall, the only remaining wall of the temple courts where Jesus taught. On the southwestern corner of the Temple Mount, the walls still lay in ruin. Yet the future story of Israel and the temple is intertwined with the time of the end.

2. The End of the Age

Jesus's reference to the end of the age has not yet been fulfilled. Both eras—the time of His generation and the time of a future generation during the end times—seem mingled in His words recorded in Mark 13.

Whether we go through calamity or the end times, we must live in the same way. Storm clouds are in this world. Every uncertainty must push us to be ready for Christ's return.

HOW WE SHOULD LIVE NOW

In His words recorded in Mark 13, Jesus said more to us about how we live now than He did of the details about the end. So what did He say about how we are to live now?

1. Be Ready and On Guard

> You must be on your guard. You will be handed over
> to the local councils and flogged in the synagogues.
> On account of me you will stand before governors
> and kings as witnesses to them. (Mark 13:9)

In this powerful sermon, Jesus closed with a message of
urgency:

> Therefore keep watch because you do not know when
> the owner of the house will come back—whether
> in the evening, or at midnight, or when the rooster
> crows, or at dawn. If he comes suddenly, do not let
> him find you sleeping. What I say to you, I say to ev-
> eryone: "Watch!" (Mark 13:35–37)

2. Do Not Be Deceived

> Jesus said to them: "Watch out that no one deceives
> you. Many will come in my name, claiming, 'I am he,'
> and will deceive many." (Mark 13:5–6)

> At that time if anyone says to you, "Look, here is the
> Messiah!" or, "Look, there he is!" do not believe it.
> For false messiahs and false prophets will appear and
> perform signs and wonders to deceive, if possible,
> even the elect. (Mark 13:21–22)

In these confusing and complex times, we must beware of

man's expertise and clever promises. We must focus on the truth of God's Word and not be deceived by false teachers.

3. Do Not Be Alarmed and Do Not Panic

Sometimes we panic over small things in our lives, not to mention the global circumstances and events that may seem to be ushering in the end of the world. Whether the city of Jerusalem is being attacked or the Second Coming is imminent, we live the same.

> When you hear of wars and rumors of wars, do not be alarmed. Such things must happen, but the end is still to come. (Mark 13:7)

Jesus taught that we must keep calm and carry on. Be still and know that He is God. Trust and obey.

4. Believe That God Is in Control

Difficult things do happen and will happen in this life. The world does seem to hit us with tough situations at a faster and faster rate every day. Life can be overwhelming. In His message about the end times, Jesus said, "Such things must happen" (Mark 13:7).

Yet God is in control today. This truth can help us right now.

5. Observe the Signs in Mark 13

In Mark 13, Jesus listed several signs of the end times that we will be able to observe as we see the days drawing closer to His return.

Tension. There will be geopolitical tension, including great international upheaval. There will be millions of refugees.

Tectonics. There will be earthquakes and an unusual level of the shifting of the crust of the earth. But these things are not the end.

Tsunamis. There will be multiple disasters, floods, and famines of biblical proportions. But these are also not the end but just the beginning of the end. The next tsunami or famine is worthy of our intense attention and giving of relief, but it is not the end of the world itself.

Terrors. There will be a terrible persecution of Christians. This persecution will be more intense than even what occurred in the first century. Christians seem to be experiencing increased danger in these days. Each year seems to be bringing more persecution.

Pray that the Lord will give us the words to speak. We must not flinch when under such pressure. We must be wise and live at peace. But may each of us be ready to speak for Jesus even if it endangers our lives. We will suffer for Him. Let us not shrink back or be ashamed.

Luke's Gospel records Jesus using powerful language to describe the end times:

> There will be signs in the sun, moon and stars. On the earth, nations will be in anguish and perplexity at the roaring and tossing of the sea. People will faint from terror, apprehensive of what is coming on the world, for the heavenly bodies will be shaken. (21:25–26)

6. *Tell It*

Jesus said that before He returns, the gospel will be preached.

> And the gospel must first be preached to all nations. (Mark 13:10)

Discussing the rebuilding of the temple is worthy. But not every crisis is the crisis that means the end is near. We must distinguish between the many anti-Christs and the Antichrist.

Jesus focused on the gospel. It is always time to obey the Great Commission, especially in the end times. Every crisis is a call to preach, win, send, and reach. There will be an end-time harvest of souls—an unusually effective spreading of the Word, making disciples, and growing the church. Oh, may we respond aright!

7. *Don't Be Timid*

Despite the opportunities before us, many will fear and fail to stand strong in their faith. Remember that at the end of Jesus's life, the disciples started buckling. Judas betrayed Him; Peter was reduced to fearful denial; Mark ran away. And today many are so addicted to fear and the approval of others that they choose the easy way over the way of the cross. Many will desert the faith. It begins with watering it down. It continues with compromise, and it ends in denial.

I had to choose as I followed the Lord whether I would please Him or the crowd. God will supply courage and perseverance for His people despite betrayal and family deception.

Brother will betray brother to death, and a father his child. Children will rebel against their parents and have them put to death. Everyone will hate you because of me, but the one who stands firm to the end will be saved. (Mark 13:12–13)

Before the end times, Christians will be hated. In fact, some of us already are! Get over the fear of the world quickly. The world will hate the messengers, but we must be bold in sharing the gospel. Do not water down the truth of the Word. There is only one way to heaven—and that is through faith in Jesus Christ.

Proclaiming the uniqueness of Jesus will make many people angry. Yet His way is the very thing that saves us. Jesus died as the ransom for all. Some tragically reject the only way whereby we can be saved. Worldliness is repelled by spiritual living. So we must stand firm. In Mark 13, Jesus said that in the last days there will be an abomination (v. 14), distress (v. 19), false prophets (v. 22), and even a cosmic collapse (vv. 24–25).

The signs have always been present, but in the end there will be an accentuation of these things.

8. Believe That He Will Return

But how will it all happen? What about the rebuilding of the temple, the mark of the beast, the two end-time witnesses, and the unfulfilled prophecies yet to come of the kings of the North and South? What about the prophecies in the book of Daniel? Yes, there is more to it.

This is where Jesus leads us, quoting Daniel:

At that time people will see the Son of Man coming in clouds with great power and glory. And he will send his angels and gather his elect from the four winds, from the ends of the earth to the ends of the heavens. (Mark 13:26–27)

We must all focus on Jesus coming back.

SIGNS OF HIS RETURN

Are there any recent signs that indicate that we could be the generation that sees the return of Jesus Christ? Here are some suggestions.

1. The Deadliest Wars of All Time

Always there have been wars, slaughters, and large numbers dying on battlefields. I am writing this during the hundred-year anniversary of World War I. Though the onset of the Iron Age and the invention of the chariot increased the horrors of war, the Battle of the Somme was considered by some to be the first day of "modern warfare." The tank made its entry like the chariot of the Egyptians. This was to be the war that ended all wars.

Then Hitler's Blitzkrieg in 1939 shattered earlier knowledge of trench warfare. Attacks that previously took months were accomplished in hours. Holland fell in four days. Weaponry became more and more destructive. By 1945, forty million people had died in World War II. The same year unleashed the atomic bomb first in Hiroshima then Nagasaki. The destruction was horrific, speeding up the surrender of Japan. Was it just terrible enough to warn us never to use one again?

We had entered the era of the Cold War and the "mutually assured destruction" of the powers with such weapons. For the first time mankind could destroy itself.

2. The Most Destructive Weapons of All Time

When the *Enola Gay* dropped the atomic bomb over Hiroshima, World War II effectively ended, but a new fear came over the world. Were we going to see the end of the world in biblical proportions? We came close in 1962 with the Cuban Missile Crisis. During that time, surely only the restraining hand of God kept us safe. President Kennedy's predecessors had made it clear that a nuclear war would eliminate the entire population of the Northern Hemisphere. At one point during this state of high alert, sixty nuclear-armed American bombers remained constantly in the air.

The Cold War officially ended in 1989 when communism finally failed to hold on to the hearts and minds of the people of the old Soviet Union. The ultimate secular experiment failed. But the world remains dangerous.

3. Multiple Trouble Spots

There have always been troubles in the world. But modern weaponry and the proliferation of weapons of mass destruction raise alarm for us frequently.

Two atomic bombs having been dropped does not mean that the unleashing of a device is necessarily the end. But always pray for protection against the catastrophic loss of life. The end of the world will have mass destruction.

At the time of this writing, Russia is invading the Ukraine. The biblical nation of Israel has its troubles. There is unrest in Iraq, Syria, and North Korea. And terrorism is a dark cloud over the world. We shudder at the increased power of what we call rogue states. But God is especially interested in how the church does, in the church prevailing.

4. The Re-creation of the State of Israel in 1948

Many believe that Jeremiah 29:14 has at least in part been fulfilled.

> "I will be found by you," declares the LORD, "and will bring you back from captivity. I will gather you from all the nations and places where I have banished you," declares the LORD, "and will bring you back to the place from which I carried you into exile."

On May 12, 1948, Israel became a nation again. The United States recognized it and has stood with Israel ever since.

This tiny nation, the size of New Jersey, is surrounded by Islamic nations—nations that together have a landmass the size of the United States plus a million square miles more! Israel is hated. But against all odds, it remains the only democracy in the region and a sought-after land. Many believe the establishment of Israel is another catalytic end-time event, perhaps mirrored in the verse given above.

5. Moral Decline, Deception, and Decadence

> But mark this: There will be terrible times in the last days. People will be lovers of themselves, lovers of money, boastful, proud, abusive, disobedient to their parents, ungrateful, unholy, without love, unforgiving, slanderous, without self-control, brutal, not lovers of the good, treacherous, rash, conceited, lovers of pleasure rather than lovers of God—having a form of godliness but denying its power. (2 Timothy 3:1–5)

We seem to be living in such days. The formerly Christian West appears today to be more secular and even pagan.

6. The Gospel Is Being Preached

The church used to hinge on the United States and Western Europe. Now we truly have a global church.

The story is not over for the West, but the huge increase in Christ-followers globally has been in Asia, Africa, and South America. The church is not yet finished in the Middle East either. We have seen before that the blood of the martyrs is the seed of the church, so good stories continue to emerge from that region. Nations in the Middle East that had virtually no Christians thirty years ago now have thousands of believers. I rely on missionaries for these carefully told stories as it is hard and even dangerous to quantify, yet the evidence is strong that the church is overcoming. But the world has yet to see the greatest move of God before Christ returns.

It is still time to call men and women, boys and girls in all cultures to repent and believe in Jesus. The task is unfinished with, some say, six thousand people groups yet to hear in their own language.

The church must never be a cul-de-sac for the Great Commission, with no roads leading outward. One of the great tragedies is that the church can lose its mission so easily, and it becomes about us. If your faith is growing, why not help another person? You may even use this book to help others with doubts. Tell them not to be bullied by their doubts. We are free to believe.

7. Demonic Evil Unleashed

Has there been a greater evil in history than the Holocaust? If ever there was a film to ignore the R-rating and watch, it is *Schindler's List*. Steven Spielberg did well to help many remember what evil wants us to forget. Nazi Germany deliberately murdered six million Jews between 1939 and 1945.

We live in an era when millions have been killed. Hundreds of thousands of Christians are being killed each year for their faith. This could be an end-time evil. We are seeing a change in Western morality as marriage is cherished less and less, good is called evil, and evil is called good.

8. Instant Worldwide Communications

CNN, FOX News, and the BBC may or may not capture Jesus's appearance when He returns. But the Bible says that every eye will see Him (Revelation 1:7). We must make no assumptions about how. I will be surprised, though, if the

Antichrist is not media savvy. We can see that the technological revolution in the last hundred years has added to the intensity of the days we live in.

Signs of the last days abound. But remember: the signs are not the end. Signposts point us in the right direction, give us warnings, and encourage us to stay on the right road.

There is great complexity to this world and to the culmination of history. The book of Revelation and other end-times prophecy can seem quite complicated. But it's simple: Jesus is coming back, and we better be ready. There is always an urgency in the heart of the Christian balanced with contentment. My sense is that we often need to be reminded more to wake up.

As Peter said:

The Lord is not slow in keeping his promise, as some understand slowness. Instead he is patient with you, not wanting anyone to perish, but everyone to come to repentance.

But the day of the Lord will come like a thief. The heavens will disappear with a roar; the elements will be destroyed by fire, and the earth and everything done in it will be laid bare.

Since everything will be destroyed in this way, what kind of people ought you to be? You ought to live holy and godly lives. (2 Peter 3:9–11)

ARE YOU READY?

Many great studies have been written on the subject of the end times. Such study is worthy. When I was in seminary, I studied apocalyptic (end-times) literature. I am advocating neither arrogance nor ignorance in regard to this subject.

But when all is said and done, that fifteen-year-old boy who taught that simple Bible study many years ago was close to the truth—Jesus is coming back. We better be ready! We need to live with a sense of gospel urgency and personal readiness. Throughout my years of ministry, I have tried never to lose that sense of urgency. We don't know the day that He shall return. So you and I should always be ready.

Are we ready? Are we living in expectation of His coming? Is what is on your computer at this moment something that is pleasing to the Judge of all the living and the dead? Is the way you treat your spouse, neighbors, and church ready for Judgment Day? Have you used your resources for yourself or for God? Have you been following Jesus, or are you asking Jesus to follow you?

Have you conquered prejudice? In heaven we shall all live in the same subdivision—or rather in the same no-division!

Are you turning from the sins and idols of the day, and are you living for Christ? Is your urgency for the gospel the kind that pleases our crucified, risen, and returning Lord? Are you living generously?

In fact, we must always live as if Jesus could return this very hour. Jesus is coming back. We better be ready!

Every eye will see Him, and for the believer, the Bridegroom will have come. Nothing will ever be the same. Pull out that telescope by reading the Scriptures—and don't doubt that He is on His way to bring His people home.

CONCLUSION

A NEW PERSPECTIVE

Thank you for journeying with me in the pages of this book. Though these words of mine answering the seven great questions are in so many ways not up to the task, these seven truths are perfect. These truths are what we need for the journey that lasts for eternity.

The facts are certain and sure. They tell the story of the gospel. They make sense of this life and help us get ready for what's next. Build your life on God's truth. Teach your children. Win those who have never heard or who are far from God.

These words do only small justice to these seven questions, these critical themes. But let me tell you, the truths are great. Believe all seven—all of God's truth.

So how are your doubts?

I hope that you have looked through the lens of each section of this book and that you can see more clearly now that there are answers to your questions. Now that you have viewed reality through the telescope of the seven truths we have put together in this book, maybe you can see that life began in a reasonable fashion. Maybe design does make sense. And maybe God's design means that He has left instructions that help life work better.

And if God has revealed Himself in history, perhaps there is a true record of it rooted in real-life events.

And maybe this record of Scripture helps us focus on the truth that Christ was born, lived, and died for sinners.

And if He did that, then we can know Him, we shall see Him, and He is coming back.

Why just believe one section? Put together all the seven truths you have learned in this book. Believe all of it. Gaze at the truth and let it be forever in view. Say good-bye to doubt. Troubles will come and bring great pain. But when we see the truth, our perspective is all together different. We look ahead. We are restored. We hope again.

Thomas, the disciple of Jesus, once doubted. He was miserable. Then he believed, and his despair turned to joy. Now you and I must also run this race mapped out for us. I hope that you are convinced.

However, if you aren't sure that you have believed in Jesus Christ for the forgiveness of your sin, there is a way you can be sure.

The problem of sin in the world is everyone's problem. The Bible clearly states the problem: all of us have sinned and fallen short of God's glory (Romans 3:23). Thankfully, the Bible also invites us to experience the solution. We can have faith today. The Bible explains that we must repent, believe, and receive the gift of eternal life found in Jesus (Acts 2:38, John 3:16-17).

I encourage you to personalize this. Why not pray this prayer now where you are, as you dedicate yourself to the One this book is all about?

> *Dear Father,*
> *I admit that I share the same problem as everyone else: I have sinned against You. So I repent of my sins.*
> *Thank You that Jesus died on the cross for my sins. I believe in You, Jesus, that You are the Son of God who died and rose again.*
> *I receive the gift of Your Spirit and ask that I may be filled with joy as I follow and obey You the rest of my life.*

Now, don't doubt. Believe. Get a Bible and read it. Join a local church and obey God. He will never let you down.

If you have prayed that prayer and given your life to Christ, one day you and I will see each other in heaven. Together, we will believe and follow the Lord Jesus Christ, the beginning and the end. No doubt about it!

ACKNOWLEDGMENTS

First, many thanks to my assistant, Valencia Marierose, for serving New Hope with cheerful energy and powerful prayer support.

To our New Hope team, many of whom have been with us from the beginning: Tim and Suzanne Woodruff, Al and Shelly Mead, Joe and Tammy Pritchett, John and Donna Conrad, Hugh and Mary Lynn Kirby, Libby and Jerry Baker, and our home group, including Lesley and Steve Deyton, and Jon and Mandy Huff. To Josh and Leigh Anne Harwell, Clark and Selina Dailey, your creative input is remarkable. I want to give a big thanks to all the staff!

I must say a special thanks to those I call upon as a prayer team and uphold me so often.

Thank you to Kelli Sallman, my first editor who has outstanding gifts. Thank you to Phil Kelly for recommending Kelli. Thank you to Eleanor Stenner for being the first to read through and make lots of helpful suggestions and corrections.

Special thanks to all at Worthy: Byron Williamson, Leeanna Nelson, Caroline Green, Nicole Pavlas, Jeanna Ledbetter, and Jennifer Stair. Your input is remarkable and done in such positive, intelligent, and spiritual fashion.

This book followed after a series of connections, encouragements, and the occasional round of golf. One relay of connection goes from Ike Rieghard, the greatest of encouragers, to Jay Strack to Hank Hanegraaff ("The Bible Answer Man"), back to Jay Strack and to my incredible agent, Ted Squires. I am so thankful for your wisdom and insightful counsel.

Thank you, Ken Ham, for your added critical thinking and support.

I have a long list of pastors I would love to thank, many of whom have endorsed this book. Let me also add thanks to Danny Forshee, David Mackinley, Keith Moore, and Jim Thomas.

Thanks to all my family in the UK, especially my mum, who already has a much more successful published author with my sister, Sophie Duffy.

To my brother, Peter, who is mentioned in the second sentence in this book. I could never get a word in! I am proud of you.

I am thankful for Tom Daniel, now with the Lord, whom I know would love the first chapter; Derek Tidball, my highly valued mentor; Steve Brady; and Phillip Deuk, the most faithful of friends.

To our Brighton family: Graham and Margaret, Keith and Sheila, Sean and Ali, Mike and Sarah, Tina and Tony, and David and Laura.

Thanks to our American family: Rich and Vicki and all your clan, John and Donna and your family, Larry Reeves, Ray Gardner, Rosemary Preston, and Meg Groce.

To our Wales partners: Andy and Viv, Dale and Helen, Ellis and Kerry, Dave and Jean, Andy and Jan, and John and Debbie. And to the world of rugby: Garin Jenkins, Emyr Lewis, Chris Jones, Byron Hayward, Nigel Meek, and Dai Morris.

Special long-term thanks for the life investment from Ian Burley, Don Boykin, Dan Cathy, Mark de Moss, Steve Kenny, Mike Wolf, Robbie Baggett, and Randy Weaver.

To Bob, Linda, and Elena Dukes. Thank you for a place of refuge.

Thank you to Al Shaw for leading me to the One this book is all about.

Glory to the One and Only.

? STUDY GUIDE

If in doubt . . . you are in the right place! Doubts are welcome in Christianity because Christianity can stand up to doubts. Whether you are doing this study in a group or on your own, below are a few suggestions to make the discussion time safe and productive.

- PRAY for the group time. Ask God to help you understand what you discuss and to give you opportunities to share with others the truths you learn.
- EXPECT God to bless the time and effort you invest in strengthening your faith.
- LISTEN as people share their doubts. Validate their questions. Support them as they seek answers.
- SHARE THE TIME with other members of the group. An opportunity to speak is an opportunity to be listened to and feel respected, and we all like that.
- KEEP CONFIDENTIAL ALL THAT IS SHARED. What people share in the group—especially during prayer time—is not to be shared with anyone else.

INTRODUCTION
A CLEAR VIEW OF TRUTH

1. On a scale from 1 to 10—with 1 being completely at rest and 10 being a tornado—what general level of doubt do you have about your faith?

2. Why are you doing this study? Looking over the table of contents, which topic(s) do you hope to learn—or learn more—about?

This book helps answer the questions of faith, and it challenges the doubts that can be answered (2).

3. Sometimes we have "doubts of faith"—questions we must answer as we embrace the faith we grew up with or information we need as we come to faith as an adult. Other doubts result from life experiences or intellectual pursuits. Which kind(s) of doubts do you deal with?

If we are in doubt, the answers may be much nearer than we realize. But when we receive the answers, we must also be willing, like Thomas, to say that Jesus is our Lord and our God (3-4).

4. Read John 20:24–28. In what ways can you relate to the apostle Thomas in his doubt? How did Jesus respond to Thomas when he expressed doubt? How does it make you feel to know that Jesus responds the same way to you in your doubt?

Doubt can also be a very good thing. Doubt can spark valid questions and cause you to investigate issues in order to uncover the truth (4).

5. Do you think Christianity requires blind faith? Why or why not? Read Hebrews 11:1. How does the Bible define *faith*?

As we pull out the sections of the telescope with each of the following chapters, my prayer is that the truths explained in this book will answer the seven great questions that are essential for a lifetime of faith (5).

CHAPTER 1
DID GOD MAKE THE WORLD?

1. Why do you think most people no longer believe that God created the world? What is appealing about the theory of evolution?

Despite the disproof of many of the so-called evolution evidences that my generation had been fed in high school, the "fact" of evolution was widely assumed and accepted. . . . Those who questioned or debated the theory of evolution were treated as mentally weak (8).

2. Have you ever been criticized or shamed for believing that God created the world? If so, briefly explain the situation. What happened? How did you respond?

3. Why do you think many evolutionists seem to want to squelch healthy debate? Why are some people hostile to genuine inquiry?

If there is no Creator, then there is no God, no judgment, and no need for salvation in Jesus. The question "Did God create the world?" is ultimately founded on the most basic question of all: "Is there a God?" If this foundation is lost, then we lose everything (10).

4. Why is the question "Did God create the world?" essential to the Christian faith? What aspects of the Christian faith are founded on the premise that God created the world?

5. Why do you think many people scoff at the idea of design and prefer to assume that nature's complexity happened randomly?

6. Why is theistic evolution—combining the biblical truth of creation with the theory of evolution—not a valid option for Christians?

The theory of evolution claims that there is no guiding force at work in the world, directing changes in the species. All is random. Only the fittest survive. To the evolutionist, everything in this universe is a result of natural selection without a selection committee (14).

7. How does irreducible complexity contradict evolution's principle of the survival of the fittest?

Evolution says there is nothing special about humans; we are just another animal species that evolved though the natural process. In contrast, the Bible says that God created one man and one woman, and all of us are descendants from the uniquely designed First Couple. In the biblical view, men and women are the pinnacle of creation (19).

8. In what ways are humans different from animals? Read Genesis 1:27. Why is it significant that God created one man and one woman, instead of the evolutionary process producing many variants of primitive humans?

9. The anthropic principle states that conditions had to be just right in order for life on earth to exist. Which scientific facts in the section "The Wonder of the World's Design" struck you as interesting or insightful?

10. Based on the evidence you have read in this chapter, which option do you choose to explain how the universe came into existence: intelligent design or random chance? Why?

That God exists and that He made us are the most basic truths of life. We can choose either to lift up our eyes to God and recognize Him as our Maker, or we can look merely at what is materially in front of us and attribute it all to random chance. Our choice will determine our destiny (19).

CHAPTER 2
IS THERE A RIGHT AND WRONG?

1. If everything exists as a result of random chance, then how can we be sure of what is right and wrong? Who decides what is right?

2. In your own life, how do you decide what is right and wrong? What standard—or whose opinions— do you use?

3. Like a loving parent, God gives us freedom but also sets boundaries for our own protection. Do you think God's standards of right and wrong result in confining misery or greater freedom? Explain your answer.

This sense of right and wrong ultimately comes from on high. We can know right and wrong by revelation, not by random chance or the quirks of history. If creation changes everything, if the Bible is right about our origin, then we had better quickly get back to the instructions we have received from our Maker (38).

4. If there is no basis for right and wrong, then why do people usually believe certain things are wrong, such as rape, brutal violence, or murder? If everything is

permitted as long as we feel like it, then why do we have any laws?

What kind of a world would we live in if it were okay to steal, drive however fast we want to, or eat a whole package of Oreos without offering one to anyone else? The issue goes back to who decides what the standard of right and wrong is (45).

5. Evolution says there are no moral absolutes because there is no God. In light of this reasoning, explain why atheism has such a bad track record for human rights.

6. In what ways does the biblical account of God's creation help us in a discussion of ethics?

There is a standard of right and wrong: it comes from the God of the Bible (50).

7. Read Matthew 5:17. What was Jesus's attitude toward God's law—the standard of right and wrong that God revealed in the Bible?

8. Why did Jesus have to die as a sacrifice to cover our sins? What does the cross of Jesus help us understand about our world and about God?

9. What are some of the things you would include in a speaking-the-truth-in-love discussion with people who view themselves as good people, not sinners?

Each one of us has sinned and fallen short of God's perfect standard of right and wrong (Romans 3:23). . . . Jesus was sacrificed in our place. The righteous Son of God was slain not for the righteous but the undeserving (2 Corinthians 5:21). And Romans 8:1 tells us that the result of Jesus's sacrifice is there is no longer any condemnation from God for those who trust Christ (51).

10. Does saving faith in Jesus mean that we no longer have to obey God's commands? Explain.

Our freedom in Christ does not mean that we are free to do anything we want to. It means we are free to do everything God wants us to (53).

CHAPTER 3
IS THE BIBLE RELIABLE?

1. The Bible is made up of sixty-six books, written by forty authors in three languages on three continents over fifteen hundred years. Why is that fact an argument for the divine inspiration of the Bible?

2. What is "internal consistency"—and why is this characteristic of God's Word relevant in a discussion of the reliability of Scripture?

The Old Testament presents the history of Israel. . . . If the stories told in Scripture were myth, they would not have endured in the life of a nation as its core story (60-61).

3. Early Christian councils determined that in order for a letter or Gospel to be accepted into the New Testament, the writer needed to have witnessed the risen Lord and have apostolic authority. Why aren't other Gospels, such as the Gospel of Thomas, included in the New Testament?

The New Testament is also a book of real history. Like the Old Testament, the New Testament Scriptures were carefully preserved (62).

4. What is significant about the fact that most of the New Testament was written within fifty years of Jesus's resurrection and carefully preserved in a significant number of texts?

Recent archaeological discoveries have proven to be a great boost for the reliability of Bible history and Bible facts (67).

5. If you were having a discussion about the accuracy of Scripture, what facts would you mention about the Codex Sinaiticus, the Dead Sea Scrolls, and the painstaking preservation of the ancient texts?

The more discoveries that historians and archaeologists make about the ancient world, the more ground the skeptics lose. (70)

6. Review the descriptions of eight facts about the reliability of your Bible in the section "Is It All a Hoax?" In a discussion of your faith and God's Word, which one or two facts would you mention about each of them?

The Bible is reliable because Jesus is reliable. The Word cannot be separated from the One who is the Word (John 1:1) (83).

7. Do you agree or disagree with the statement "When we see the Bible, we see Jesus"? Explain your answer.

The Bible is the Magna Carta, the Declaration of Independence, the Constitution of all literature (85).

8. Read Matthew 7:24–25. What does building your life on the rock-solid foundation of Scripture mean in practical, twenty-first-century terms? How can we help each other build our lives on the rock of God's Word?

Living the way God calls us to live is not easy. But . . . when we follow the ways outlined and taught in the Bible, we can have wisdom and even find life, both abundant and eternal (85).

9. Honestly, how often do you read the Bible? In what ways are you relying on God and His Word today?

10. What can you do to help share the message of the Bible with others?

Take God at His Word. It is far superior to the latest theories and fads; it will never let you down. The Bible is utterly reliable, so build your life on the rock-solid foundation of Scripture (86).

CHAPTER 4
IS JESUS GOD?

1. Do you think Jesus is the most influential person in history? Why or why not?

2. The Bible says that every human being born since Adam and Eve has inherited Adam's sin. In this light, explain why Jesus had to be born of a virgin.

A sinful man cannot save another sinful man. Only a perfect, sinless God can save us. . . . In order to save us, Jesus had to be born as one of us, and He also had to be God (90).

3. Why is Jesus's divinity necessary for our salvation?

4. What did you learn in this chapter about the different perspectives in each of the four New Testament Gospels and how they complement each other?

It is a myth that Jesus was merely a good teacher. A good teacher would never claim to be God unless it were true. So if Jesus was not God—as He said He was—then He was either delusional or a nasty deceiver. He cannot be both good and delusional; nor can He be good and a liar. The only way for Jesus to be good is if, in fact, He is who He claimed to be (102).

5. What do we know of Jesus's life? Describe what you learned in this chapter about His childhood and His character. Why is it significant that Jesus never sinned?

6. What is your favorite miracle of Jesus, and what does it tell you about Jesus?

7. Jesus clearly and radically claimed to be God in His seven "I am" statements in the Gospel of John, listed in the section "Jesus's Claims." Which of those seven statements is most meaningful to you today? Why?

Prayer takes us deep and sends us out into the world. Prayer is a challenging journey. But no one did it better than Jesus, and He must be our teacher (104).

8. What makes prayer hard for you? What can you do to overcome those challenges?

9. Look again at the Lord's Prayer in Matthew 6:9–13. Comment on its focus points, length, order of topics, and what the aspects of this prayer suggest about Jesus's priorities in prayer.

10. Jesus was our mediator through His death and resurrection. Why do you think Christians emphasize
the cross so much?

*Scripture says, "There is one God and one mediator between God and
mankind, the man Christ Jesus" (1 Timothy 2:5). Jesus Christ is forever
our only hope and forever the only way to salvation and eternal life (108).*

CHAPTER 5
DID JESUS RISE FROM THE DEAD?

1. Naturalists believe that since miracles do not usually happen, they cannot happen. Do you agree or disagree with this logic? Explain your answer.

The biblical evidence says Jesus did rise from the dead. So the naturalists have to explain this historical evidence. Their theories of what they think really happened read like an Agatha Christie or Sherlock Holmes whodunit (111).

2. The pathetic disciples theory claims that the apostles were unintelligent and made up the resurrection story as mere wish fulfillment, a hallucination, or even a ghost or UFO sighting. What arguments from logic and reason contradict this theory?

3. The swap theory suggests that Jesus's resurrection was an elaborate con, substituting a lookalike who posed as Jesus and died on the cross, while the real Jesus hid and later appeared to the disciples, claiming to have resurrected. What are some of the problems with this theory?

4. The swoon theory claims that Jesus didn't actually die on the cross but merely swooned, later recovering

and appearing to the disciples as if He had died and risen. Why does this theory not stand up to historical evidence or logic?

All four Gospels, however, leave no room for doubt about the resurrection of Jesus Christ (118).

5. Read Matthew 16:21–23 and Matthew 20:17–19. Why is it significant that neither Jesus's death nor His resurrection took Him by surprise?

6. Why is it important that Jesus's death occurred in open view of the public, witnessed by His followers and also His opponents? Consider the evidence of Jesus's physical death on Calvary.

7. The Pharisees insisted that Romans guard Jesus's tomb. Why did the Pharisees have a vested interest in having His tomb guarded? And why did the guards have a vested interest in keeping Jesus's body in that tomb?

8. All of the apostles (except Judas) were martyred because of their faith in Jesus. Why can their deaths be considered evidence of the resurrection?

9. Ten proofs of Jesus's resurrection are presented in the section "Evidences for the Resurrection." Which proofs of Jesus's resurrection do you find most compelling? Why?

Paul's conversion shows that even the toughest skeptic can believe. None of us should rule out our own conversion. And millions more like Paul have been converted (127-28).

10. List several implications of the resurrection in your life.

Jesus Christ still resurrects once spiritually dead souls, including mine. He is still working in people's lives today (128).

CHAPTER 6
IS THERE LIFE AFTER DEATH?

1. What do you think happens to people after they die?

Heaven stops us from believing that life is all about us and what we can do. Heaven is our victory, justice, and vindication. It is God putting things right (134).

2. In what ways does the promise of heaven offer comfort and encouragement to followers of Jesus Christ?

3. Briefly review the section "Views about Life After Death." How do these views—such as nothingness, reincarnation, and ghosts—contradict the Christian hope and understanding of what the Bible says about heaven?

As believers in the Word of God, we have no doubt that whether our body dies slowly or suddenly, God is not caught by surprise. We will be resurrected even if we were beheaded, crucified, or burned like the some of the first apostles. Even if we are buried in a mass grave, cremated, or lost at sea, God will never lose a soul. Every human body perishes, but the soul is eternal (138).

4. Why do Christians believe that heaven is a place? Describe a few things you learned in this chapter about the place of heaven.

5. Heaven is also an experience. Read Revelation 21:4. According to the Bible, what will believers experience in heaven?

6. What encourages you about the fact that heaven is being with Jesus?

For many, heaven will be a great reunion; for others, it will be a million introductions. We will be able to develop each relationship to its full potential (145).

7. Heaven is filled with people. In addition to Jesus, who do you look forward to knowing in heaven? Consider people from the Bible, from history, or loved ones who are already in heaven.

Death has a finality. That is why we experience grief. There is a separation from how things were. And death brings a person to one of two destinations: either heaven by Abraham's side—or hell in agony (146).

8. For each of us death means one of two destinations: either heaven or hell. Some people say, "I would rather go to hell so I can be with my friends." Why can we conclude that there are no such relationships in hell?

Hell must be very real if the Son of God suffered an agonizing death to spare us such a fate and to give us eternity with God (147).

9. What does the Bible say about communicating with the dead? What would you say to someone who wants to communicate with a loved one who has died?

10. Are you ready to face the Lord when you die? Explain your answer.

Life is tissue paper-thin. So pray for those who are lost. Pray for the salvation of friends, relatives, and neighbors today ... and be ready yourself (151).

CHAPTER 7
IS JESUS COMING BACK?

1. Do you believe Jesus is coming back? Why or why not?

2. According to Revelation 1:7, what will Jesus's return look like? How will He return? Who will see Him?

The foundational lessons of the Second Coming come from the second person of the Trinity, the Lord Jesus Christ. He is the Creator, Sustainer, and Judge of the earth. He is the only true expert when it comes to Christ's return to earth (156).

3. Read Mark 13:32. What is the one limitation of Jesus's knowledge about His return?

4. What are some advantages of us not knowing the day and time Jesus will return? What are some disadvantages?

The subject of the end times calls for us to be trusting, humble, and zealous to do God's will. At the same time we must leave room for the mystery and sovereignty of God in all things, including the Last Days. Trusting God means going forward without knowing everything (157-58).

5. Jesus will return like "a thief in the night" (1 Thessalonians 5:2). Noticing the signs of the end times is not like reading tea leaves but more like seeing a warning light. Explain the difference between these two analogies—and the resulting difference in our behavior.

6. In Mark 13:9, Jesus calls us to be on guard. What are you doing to be ready and on guard as you anticipate His second coming?

7. What world events—and what events in your own life—may cause you to doubt God's control? What promises in Scripture, truths about God, and examples of His faithfulness to you in the past reinforce your belief that God is, indeed, in control?

8. How would you hold up under persecution for your faith in Jesus? What can you do to be prepared for such persecution?

9. What are some of the signs of the times that you learned in this chapter? Signposts like these give us warnings and encourage us to stay on the right road.

What is the right direction? What are you doing right now to walk in that direction?

There is great complexity to this world and to the culmination of history. The book of Revelation and other end-times prophecy can seem quite complicated. But it's simple: Jesus is coming back, and we better be ready (171).

10. Who comes to mind as you think of friends you could tell about Jesus? Write their names below or share them with the group. Pray for those friends before you approach them, as you talk, and after you talk as they consider what you said or—if they accepted Christ as you spoke—as they establish their newfound faith.

Jesus is coming back. We better be ready! We need to live with a sense of gospel urgency and personal readiness. . . . In fact, we must always live as if Jesus could return this very hour (172).

NOTES

CHAPTER 1: DID GOD MAKE THE WORLD?

1. Michael J. Behe, *Darwin's Black Box: The Biochemical Challenge to Evolution* (New York: Free Press, 1996), 39.

2. Ibid., 39.

3. A. R. Wallace, *Man's Place in the Universe: A Study of the Results of Scientific Research in Relation to the Unity or Plurality of Worlds*, 4th ed. (London: George Bell & Sons, 1904), 256–57.

4. Though this is all observable science, many Christian books and articles allude to these scientific facts. See, for example, Rich Deem, "The Incredible Design of the Earth and Our Solar System," www.godandscience.com; Charles Colson and Nancy Pearcey, *How Now Shall We Live?* (Carol Stream, IL: Tyndale, 1999), 59–68.

CHAPTER 2: IS THERE A RIGHT AND WRONG?

1. Joshua Straub, *Safe House* (Colorado Springs: WaterBrook, 2015), chapter 5.

2. Justin Phillips, *C. S. Lewis at the BBC: Messages of Hope in the Darkness of War* (London: HarperCollins, 2003), 120.

3. Ibid., 120.

CHAPTER 3: IS THE BIBLE RELIABLE?

1. Josh McDowell, *Evidence That Demands a Verdict*, vol. 1 (Amersham: Alpha, 1993), 69.

2. Will Heilpern, "King Hezekiah's Seal Discovered in Dump Site," CNN, December 4, 2015, http://www.cnn.com/2015/12/03/middleeast/king-hezekiah-royal-seal//.

3. Gordon Govier, "Biblical Archaeology's Top Ten Discoveries," *Christianity Today*, December 31, 2015, http://www.christianitytoday.com/ct/2015/december-web-only/biblical-archaeologys-top-ten-discoveries-of-2015.html.

4. Dan Brown, *The Da Vinci Code* (New York: Doubleday, 2003).

5. Gospel of Thomas, saying 114. As translated by Stephen J. Patterson and James M. Robinson, "The Gospel of Thomas's 114 Sayings of Jesus," Biblical Archeology Society, June 29, 2015, http://www.biblicalarchaeology.org/daily/biblical-topics/bible-versions-and-translations/the-gospel-of-thomas-114-sayings-of-jesus/.

6. John Drane, *The Bible: Fact or Fantasy* (Oxford: Lion Books, 1989), 27–33.

7. I am grateful for Josh McDowell's *Evidence That Demands a Verdict*, vol. 1 (Amersham: Alpha, 1993), 52, and Nicky Gumbel's *Questions of Life* (EastBourne: Kingsway, 1983) for emphasizing the sheer volume of Bible documents.

8. "Sennacherib's Hexagonal Prism," *Bible History Online* (2105), http://www.bible-history.com/empires/prism.html.

CHAPTER 4: IS JESUS GOD?
1. Charles Haddon Spurgeon, *Sermons on the Death and Resurrection of Jesus* (Peabody, MA: Hendrickson, 2005), 154.

CHAPTER 5: DID JESUS RISE FROM THE DEAD?
1. Thomas A. Smail, *The Forgotten Father* (Eugene, OR: Wipf and Stock, 1980), 51–52.

CHAPTER 6: IS THERE LIFE AFTER DEATH?
1. David Roach, "*Heaven Is for Real* Stirs Discussion," *Baptist Press*, April 16, 2014, http://www.bpnews.net/42386.
2. Wayne Triplett, *Heaven Is Waiting: There's No Place Like Home* (Bloomington, IN: iUniverse, 2012), 63–64.

FOR FURTHER READING

Alcorn, Randy. *Heaven*. Wheaton, IL: Tyndale, 2004.

Bickel, Bruce and Stan Jantz. *Prophecy 101*. Eugene, OR: Harvest House, 1999.

Bickersteth, John and Timothy Pain. *The Four Faces of God.,* UK: EastBourne, UK: Kingsway, 1992.

Clouse, Robert. *The Meaning of the Millennium: Four Views*. Downers Grove, IL: InterVarsity, 1977.

Colson, Charles and Nancy Pearcey. *How Now Shall We Live?* London: Marshall Pickering, 1999.

Drane, John. *The Bible: Fact or Fantasy*. Oxford: Lion Books, 1989.

Graham, Billy. *Peace with God*. London: Kingswood, 1954.

Gumble, Nicky. *Questions of Life.,* UK: EastBourne, UK: Kingsway, 1983.

Lewis, C. S. *Mere Christianity*. Great Britain: William Collins Son & Co.,1952.

Lewis, Peter. *The Glory of Christ*. London: Hodder & Stoughton, 1992.

MacArthur, John. *The Glory of Heaven*. Wheaton, IL: Crossway, 1996.

McDowell, Josh. *Evidence that Demands a Verdict*, vol. I., UK: Amersham, UK: Alpha, 1993.

Newbigin, Lesley. *The Gospel in a Pluralistic Society*. London: SPCK, 1989.

Packer, J. I. *Knowing God*. London: Hodder & Stoughton, 1973.

Smail, Tom. *The Forgotten Father*. London: Hodder & Stoughton, 1996.

Warren, Rick. *The Purpose Driven Life.,* MI: Grand Rapids, MI: Zondervan, 2002.

ABOUT THE AUTHOR

RHYS STENNER is senior pastor of New Hope Baptist Church in Fayetteville, Georgia. Originally from the United Kingdom, he attended the London School of Theology and pastored in England and ministered in Wales prior to joining New Hope. He and his wife, Louise, have three daughters and live outside Atlanta.

IF YOU ENJOYED THIS BOOK, WILL YOU CONSIDER SHARING THE MESSAGE WITH OTHERS?

Mention the book in a blog post or through Facebook, Twitter, Pinterest, or upload a picture through Instagram.

Recommend this book to those in your small group, book club, workplace, and classes.

Head over to facebook.com/worthypublishing, "LIKE" the page, and post a comment as to what you enjoyed the most.

Tweet "I recommend reading #IfInDoubt by @RhysStenner // @worthypub"

Pick up a copy for someone you know who would be challenged and encouraged by this message.

Write a book review online.

Visit us at worthypublishing.com

 twitter.com/worthypub

 worthypub.tumblr.com

 facebook.com/worthypublishing

 pinterest.com/worthypub

 instagram.com/worthypub

 youtube.com/worthypublishing